Taming Turnover

Creating Strategies for Employee Retention

Paula J. MacLean

Author of
The Supervisor's Big Book of Answers
and *Great Boards-Plain & Simple*

This book is dedicated to my friend and mentor, Carol Gillfillan, who taught me the importance of dogged optimism, the value of thinking in circles rather than straight lines, and the necessity of having both an inquiring mind and an open heart.

National Library of Canada Cataloguing in Publication Data

MacLean, Paula J., 1955-
   Taming turnover: creating strategies for employee retention

   Includes bibliographical references.
   ISBN 0-9684430-1-X

   1. Employee retention.   2. Labor turnover.   I. Title
HF5549.5.R58M32 2001   658.3'14   C2001-910462-6

1st Printing 2001
2nd Printing September 2003

Disclaimer:
The information contained in this book is intended as ideas only. The author/publisher is not providing legal or professional advice. If legal or expert advice is required, the reader is directed to seek this from a competent practitioner.   The author takes no responsibility for how information is used by the reader.   The author is also not responsible for any decisions made by the reader, nor any consequences arising from these decisions.

About the author...

Paula J. MacLean is a leading expert with 28 years experience in non-profit management, human resources, board development and governance. For the past 12 years Paula has operated her own management consulting and training enterprise, working exclusively with human service and non-profit community-based organizations. She has educated and entertained thousands of participants in workshops, courses and conferences. Paula has held positions as an executive director of a non-profit agency, a supervisor and manager, a board volunteer, and college instructor. Paula lives in Edmonton Alberta; she loves to golf and travel. She shares her life with several four-footed companions. She also claims to have some friends who walk upright!

Paula is author of three other books:

♦ **The Supervisor's Big Book of Answers** (1999) is a practical guide for supervisors and managers working in human service organizations.
♦ **Great Boards—Plain & Simple** (2003) is a must-read guidebook for managers and board volunteers in the non-profit sector.
♦ **Great Boards--Plain & Simple--The Workbook** (2003) is a practical accompaniment to *Great Boards--Plain & Simple*.

What some people have said about Paula's books...

"Her workshops cover a lot of material. But it's great to have all the detail and specifics in one handy place."

"I don't have to fly by the seat of my pants...or make it up and hope I'm not making a mistake. I can look whatever I need to up. Then add my own ideas and experience. What a relief and boost to my confidence."

"Looking up something is so quick and easy. Everything I need is in a list, in point form!"

Acknowledgements

As always, the list of people involved in a project of this nature is substantial. My thanks go to:

Linda Warford, for her thorough yet speedy literature search, and for her creativity with the book's title.

To Monika Murnane for her cover design, technical expertise, attention to detail, layout and editing.

To the many supervisors and managers in workshops, meetings and lunches who shared their turnover and recruitment frustrations and their ideas about how to improve retention.

To my parents for asking me during our Sunday telephone conversations, "How is the book coming?"   (It's finished, Mom and Dad. An autographed copy is in the mail!)

And, last but not least to Shelley, Toffee, Peaches and Partner for reminding me that talks, walks and purrs are more important than working!

How to contact us ...

By phone or fax: (780) 423-3032

By e-mail: mmcs@aol.com

Website: www.mmcs.ca

By mail: **MacLean Management Consulting
                    Services/Silver Creek Press**
                    9741 – 101A Street
                    Edmonton, Alberta
                    T5K 2R5

Discounts on bulk orders are available. Please contact us for rates. **For your convenience, order forms for** *The Supervisor's Big Book of Answers, Taming Turnover, Great Boards—Plain & Simple, and Great Boards—The Workbook* **are included at the back of this book.**

TABLE OF CONTENTS

How to use this book

This book has been written as a practical tool kit of strategies to help supervisors and managers improve employee retention. The 55 strategies begin in Part 2, Chapter 4.

Chapters 1 and 2 help you get acquainted with:

➠ the causes of turnover

➠ what defines a quality workplace, and

➠ the key factors researchers have identified as having the greatest impact on employee retention.

Chapter 3 leads you through a step by step process to:

➠ define turnover

➠ gather turnover information

➠ analyze your "turnover picture", and

➠ estimate your turnover costs.

The 55 strategies in Chapters 4 through 7 are grouped into four specific areas:

➠ recruitment and selection strategies

➠ orientation strategies

➠ supervisory strategies

➠ managerial strategies.

In short form, here are each of the 55 strategies:

1. Look in different places for applicants.
2. Look further afield.
3. Ask current employees for referrals.
4. Attend public events and community functions to network and recruit.
5. Treat recruitment as an ongoing, rather than position-specific activity.
6. Host open houses, special community events and job fairs
7. Create your own internal headhunter program.
8. Develop a partnership with local high schools for volunteer and/or work placement programs.
9. Develop a recruitment package and video.
10. When you advertise - be creative!
11. Maximize use of technology for getting the word out.
12. Speed-up your recruitment process.
13. Create realistic job previews.
14. Screen for quality not just for qualifications.
15. Interview and select for skill.
16. Interview and select for talent.
17. Partner with other organizations to share recruitment activities.
18. Assess how "coachable" an applicant is.
19. Never, never, never …
20. Apply principle-based analysis of information obtained during interviews and reference checks.
21. Start creating connections before the commencement date.

22. Involve shorter-term employees in briefing new employees about what to expect.

23. Create an orientation treasure hunt.

24. Create a buddy system for new employees.

25. Ensure regular check-ins with the new employee's supervisor.

26. Be on high alert for problems; practice early intervention.

27. Emphasize early skill-focused training.

28. Make stress management training mandatory for all new employees.

29. Provide part-time, casual, relief and contract or seasonal workers with a full orientation.

30. Evaluate and revise your orientation process at least once a year.

31. Ensure all supervisors and managers develop competence and confidence.

32. Build strong relationships, bonds and trust among employees at all levels.

33. Create a mentoring program.

34. Work toward supporting family life and work life as parts of a whole.

35. Treat every person as special and different.

36. Look for opportunities for employee input into decisions that affect them.

37. Set high, clear, achievable expectations.

38. Be creative and generous with positive feedback, recognition and rewards.

39. Respond to performance problems quickly, supportively and professionally.

40. Develop a strong support network among employees.
41. Involve employees in developing operating guidelines for their work site, team or department.
42. Enrich jobs, offer challenges and encourage skill development.
43. Offer training in 3 key areas: stress management, problem solving and conflict resolution.
44. Embrace and celebrate diversity.
45. Create a healthy, safe, and efficient working environment.
46. Include employee retention in annual operational and long range strategic planning.
47. Survey employee satisfaction regularly.
48. Focus on why employees are staying (not leaving).
49. Review policies and practices - remove barriers and improve flexibility.
50. Create specific strategies for part-time, relief, casual, and isolated employees.
51. Create improvements for women with preschool aged children.
52. Create an organization-wide training plan.
53. Manage change effectively.
54. Invest in career development.
55. Make a habit of asking for feedback – learn to listen.

Part 1

Employee Turnover:
Causes, Analysis, and
Research

The Emerging Crisis of Employee Turnover

Chapter 1

The greatest resource of any organization is its employees. A significant percentage of every organization's operating budget is devoted to recruiting, orienting, compensating, training and supervising personnel. Employees are the key to quality service and are a crucial link to achieving organizational results.

Over the past decade in my role as a management consultant and employee trainer, hundreds of managers and supervisors have peppered me with questions about how they can increase morale and job satisfaction and decrease employee turnover. Although managers have had concerns about turnover for several years, recently the issue has reached crisis proportions.

As I traveled and listened to employees, supervisors and managers of the sixty or so organizations I serve each year, several patterns emerged. Things seemed to be getting worse. Managers who had bemoaned turnover rates of 20 or 25 percent now reported rates exceeding 40 percent. Some cited specific program areas, departments or positions where turnover rates exceeded 100 percent. Once confined to smaller organizations and smaller communities, the turnover problem had grown to include multi-million dollar employers located in larger urban centres.

There was also general concern about the shrinking number of applicants responding to advertised positions. Fewer and fewer applicants had even the most rudimentary qualifications for the positions available. One supervisor described her key hiring criteria as anyone who had "two feet and a heart beat"!

"The first rule of holes is: when you are in one, stop digging."
Unknown

Finally, many managers and supervisors believed there was very little they, or their organizations, could do to improve the situation. Some believed the problem was caused primarily by low wages, poor benefits and by a society that does not value the work employees do. Frustrated and discouraged, these managers were at a loss to discover what could be done to solve a very costly problem.

Some managers connected high turnover rates to a shortage of qualified and quality applicants. Many cited employee "flaws" such as low skill level, poor work ethic, limited education and a "what's in it for me" attitude as factors precipitating employee dismissals and resignations.

<u>High Turnover Affects Everyone</u>

The impact of turnover and a shortage of qualified employees is felt at all levels inside an organization. Managers are concerned about quality of service and increased risk to clients/customers and employees. They also cite concern about rising costs for recruitment, basic training, lost productivity, and sick leave taken by over-worked remaining employees.

Supervisors are spending disproportionate amounts of time recruiting, orienting and training newly hired under-qualified or unqualified employees. Many supervisors are also pressed into doing direct client/customer service when vacant positions are not filled promptly. They report being increasingly unable to fulfill their important supervisory job duties such as giving guidance and supporting employee problem solving. Some supervisors are reluctant to deal with an employee's performance problems because they fear giving critical feedback or disciplinary action will cause the employee to resign.

Full-time and part-time employees are expected to work more overtime, undesirable shifts on nights or weekends and often in jobs, programs or departments with which they are unfamiliar.

Last, but certainly not least, clients/customers are impacted by employee turnover. They may experience lack of service consistency, communication breakdown, decreased employee morale, and mistakes made by new employees.

Are Wages and Benefits the *Primary* Problem?

In sectors where low wages and minimal benefits are the norm, many managers believe this to be "the problem" causing high turnover and difficulty in recruiting qualified personnel. However, there is substantial research evidence which suggests employees value the *quality* of a workplace as much or more than the money they earn or the benefits available.

"We don't have the money, so we'll have to think."

Unknown

This is not to suggest that wages and benefits are *unimportant.* It merely points to the importance of factors such as support from supervisors and coworkers, job flexibility, autonomy, involvement in decision-making and role clarity as crucial for creating a stable, happy workforce.

Research Literature Gives Us Some Clues

Several studies point out managers tend to emphasize external factors beyond their control (e.g. revenue or funding, low wages, competition, small pools of qualified candidates, and employee personal/family needs) as reasons for turnover and recruitment problems.

Secondly, some managers and employees have differing opinions about why employees leave a workplace.   Ahead of wages, employees cited internal organizational conditions

"There are no hopeless situations; there are only people who have grown hopeless about them."

Clare Boothe Luce

such as supervisor and co-worker support, flexibility, interesting work, recognition and opportunities to learn and be challenged.   Notably, these factors are within managers' ability to influence or directly control.

Finally, many studies identified compensation as *a* factor but not always as *the primary* factor influencing employee retention. These findings suggest managers' perceptions of why people leave are sometimes out of sync with what employees say influence their decisions to resign.

Clearly, if managers misperceive the causes of turnover, they:

➠ may believe no action is possible and

➠ are more likely to choose strategies that have little or no impact on the problem.

We will explore the role of compensation and other factors more fully in our review of recent research literature in Chapter 2.

Getting Clarity - Would the *Real Issue* Please Stand-Up?

In the popular 1970's game show "To Tell the Truth" a panel of celebrities asked questions of each of three contestants in an attempt to identify the contestant who was really who she/he claimed to be. Turnover also masquerades in several different identities.

Turnover is an Indicator of Workplace Quality

High turnover is not the *real* issue or problem. Instead, high turnover is an *indicator* of a problem. As the saying goes, people "vote with their feet". Workplaces that meet employees' needs for belonging, challenge, safety, significance, support and guidance are likely to retain more employees. Workplaces that have one or several of these key elements missing are likely to experience higher turnover.

Fundamentally then, employee turnover (or successful *employee retention* as we will soon reframe it) is a measure of the *quality* of a workplace in many different domains. A stable workforce (i.e. one where turnover is low) is likely indicative of supervisors and managers doing many things right.

Some managers have come to regard turnover as unavoidable. Clearly not all turnover can be avoided. Indeed some turnover is necessary and desirable. However, improved employee retention is crucial for many employers. Creating a stable workforce requires activities be directed at improving the quality of working life.

> *Employee retention doesn't happen by accident; it happens by plan.*

Successful employee retention is a result of deliberate and targeted strategies on a number of different fronts. It won't happen if we have a singular focus (e.g. on wages and benefits). It also won't happen if we accept turnover as an inevitable cost of doing business.

Turnover vs. Retention

Language not only shapes thoughts and ideas, it helps create organizational cultures. The majority of managers and supervisors and also the research literature, focus on discussions of *turnover*. The reverse side of the coin, and indeed the goal of this book, is employee *retention*. Attending to turnover rather than retention has a number of possible implications. First, it causes us to focus on *the problem* (people are leaving us) and *the diagnosis* (why are they leaving?) rather than on *the solutions* (what do we do to help them stay?). Secondly, we report negative statistics (we have 35 percent turnover) rather than positive statistics (we have 65 percent retention). Finally, we look in the wrong places for ideas for improvement – often by interviewing employees who are leaving.

What's Wrong with Exit Interviews?

On the surface, there is nothing wrong with conducting exit interviews. They have long been recommended practice by human resource courses and texts. However, interviewing exiting employees has several limitations.

First, exit interviews are often conducted by a supervisor or manager who has some direct responsibility for the employee who is leaving. This may not create a safe environment for the employee to give complete and honest feedback.

Secondly, no matter who is conducting the interview, most employees know it is not in their best interest to burn their bridges with a soon-to-be former employer. They may need a reference in the future. They may want to return as an employee in the future. As an employee of another organization, they may be required to work with their former coworkers.

Thirdly, exiting employees often identify unresolved issues or problems (some of which are already known to managers), but rarely do they present solutions. They have little vested interest in working through the issue since they have made their decision to leave. They may also be exhausted from trying to fix problems and are therefore reluctant to discuss the situation further. In short, they have a low investment in helping the organization improve.

Finally, some managers or supervisors may have a tendency to not address the issues presented by employees during their exit interview. Employee feedback may be minimized because it comes from a disgruntled or "uncommitted" ex-employee.

Who is Staying and Why? - A Better Approach

Interviewing or surveying current employees gives insights that can be readily turned into strategies to improve the quality of the workplace. It is in their *best interest* to help supervisors and managers improve things. Asking employees what is going right and what could be improved, engages them in a process of consultation and reinforces that their employer cares about them. We are asking our best people to be our partners in problem solving, not just problem finding!

After You Ask – You Must Act

If managers and supervisors accept that employees know what would help them stay, then we are compelled to act to improve the quality of the workplace. It requires us to listen and influence things to change inside our organizations. It demands that we look openly and self-critically at policies, practices, culture and customs for what can be done to improve retention. Employee empowerment is often discussed. This is the ultimate test of our resolve to involve employees in organizational improvement.

When we ask for input from employees we must be prepared to do something about the comments and ideas we receive. In fact, we are much more accountable for following up on suggestions with current employees than we are with exiting employees.

This does not mean that every employee's ideas are sound, viable or cost effective. It *does* mean that over time, employees must be able to point to workplace improvements reflecting their suggestions.

Having Satisfied Employees is Not an Option – It's A *Must*

Contemporary organizations and the managers who lead

For the first time ever, we need the employee more than they need us.

them, are increasingly driven by a set of key principles or values. Striving to serve clients/customers, maintain financial stability, improve outcomes and attain goals may sometimes leave employees feeling they are in a secondary role.

Long hours, demanding work, limited recognition, inadequate compensation, high workloads, authoritarian supervisors, rigid policies, job-site isolation and lack of support contribute to employee stress and dissatisfaction. Dissatisfied employees are more likely to treat clients/customers and each other badly. They are also more likely to dislike their leaders and to break policies they regard as unreasonable or unnecessary. The result is decreased morale and increased turnover. Worse yet, because the organization has earned a reputation as being a below-average employer, it will experience difficulty in filling vacant positions.

Reasonable hours, diverse and personalized forms of recognition, support of co-workers and supervisors, new challenges and control over job tasks (as well as dozens of other factors to be discussed later in this book) will improve employee satisfaction. Satisfied employees are more likely to treat customers/clients and each other well. They are also likely to become emissaries for the organization, making it an attractive employer to future job applicants.

Creating a positive environment takes work and diligence over a period of years. This work is not about giving in to employees' every whim. What is necessary is:

➠ sincere and long term efforts to listen to employees

➠ policies and practices that guide without being rigid

➠ fair treatment of employees

➠ training that is both needed and wanted.

Turnover Rates Reflect Manager's & Supervisor's Approaches

In their recent book *"First Break All the Rules"* (1999), authors Cunningham and Coffman, note their research confirms people do not leave an organization or employer, *they leave their supervisor or manager.* At its very foundation then, turnover is a reflection of the actions of managers and supervisors.

The new Golden Rule is: As you treat your employees, so will they treat your clients/customers.

Consider two teams within one organization that experience very different turnover or retention rates. Rates differ despite the fact both operate within the same policies, with similar job expectations, client/customer challenges and financial resources. The manager or supervisor of each group sets the tone, provides the support, clarifies expectations, and helps solve problems. Retention rates are directly affected by these different approaches, actions and decisions of managers. (Buckingham and Coffman, 1999).

Managers and supervisors must be actively involved in the development and implementation of retention programs. Senior managers, organizational policies, resources and employee development practices must actively support manager's and supervisor's retention efforts. In turn, senior leaders must hold managers and supervisors accountable for turnover of employees in their work units.

Action to Improve Retention is Crucial

We live in a time of increasing public demand for quality services. Service quality is maximized when employees enjoy their work and are supported to do their jobs well. Employees are our key resource, linked inextricably to customer/client satisfaction and therefore, to organizational success. Retaining them is not an option, it is an imperative.

"Nothing great has ever been achieved without enthusiasm."

Ralph Waldo Emerson

Equally as compelling is the need to decrease the number of employees who must be recruited. This reduces hard costs related to hiring, as well as the less obvious costs associated with disruption in service quality, productivity and increased stress experienced by remaining employees after a co-worker resigns.

What Can Be Done To Improve Employee Retention?

Despite some managers' beliefs to the contrary, much can be done to create workplaces that attract and retain quality employees. Later in *Taming Turnover* we will explore:

- how to define and measure avoidable turnover

- how to set reasonable retention targets

- creative recruitment strategies that will help you get a "good hire"

- the best orientation strategies to ensure a new employee successfully completes the first few months on the job

- 55 powerful strategies for supervisors and managers to use to improve retention.

The Human Resource Manager's Role

If your organization is fortunate enough to have a human resource manager, it is important to dedicate some of his/her time to retention activities. At present, your HR manager's time is likely fully committed to a range of recruitment activities and to coordinating training for new and existing employees. Making retention a top priority means less turnover. Less turnover means less time spent recruiting, orienting and conducting base training for new staff.

The Importance of Having a Plan for Employee Retention

Take a quick look at the annual operating budget or most recent financial statements of your organization. What percentage of your resources is spent on wages, benefits, recruitment, orientation and training? In many customer/client service focused organizations this percentage is at least 80 percent and may be as high as 90 percent. This means employees are not only our most important resource, they also represent our biggest annual operating expense.

> *"If you fail to plan, you are planning to fail."*
> Unknown

As managers and supervisors we have been diligent in creating personnel policies, benefit policies, training programs, orientation checklists, interview questions, reference check questions and many other important pieces of paper. However, very few organizations have a *deliberate, written, targeted, strategic plan* for keeping good employees working for and with them over the long term. Instead, we leave this to chance. If they stay, we say, "Great!" If they leave, we say, "Oh well, there's not much we could have done; after all, it's the employee's decision, not ours."

Retention is a Result of Good Management Practices

"Good management" is rarely the result of abundant resources or the academic credentials of managers. It is pre-eminently a matter of relationships, trust, integrity, communication, appreciation of people and understanding their talents. In simple terms, it is not solely about *what* supervisors and managers do, it is also about *how* they do it.

> *By what and who they put first and last, supervisors and managers set the tone of a workplace.*

My earlier book, *The Supervisor's Big Book of Answers* (1999), is recommended reading for all supervisors and managers. Following the step by step guides in *The Supervisor's Big Book of Answers* will help you make significant improvements in workplace quality. As we will see later, the quality of supervision provided to employees is key to creating a stable workforce of challenged and satisfied employees.

Perhaps the most important challenge is listening to and involving employees in helping create workplaces that draw people in, guide, support and challenge them, and ultimately make them feel they belong and are significant.

> *"When we know better, we must do better."*
> Unknown

Employee Turnover: Research, Causes & Cures

Chapter *2*

What Defines a Quality Workplace?

Let's begin by defining *workplace.* A workplace is clearly not only the physical site or facilities housing employees during their working day. The workplace includes all of the conditions and interactions created by an employer. The *quality* of the workplace therefore includes facilities *plus* factors such as:

➠ clarity of role and job expectations

➠ quality and quantity of supervision available

➠ co-worker support

➠ flexibility of tasks and scheduling

➠ communication practices

➠ recognition for work done well

➠ training and development activities

➠ wages and benefits

➠ opportunities to participate in decision-making

➠ variety of work and challenges on the job.

General Themes and Focus

The literature focuses on three main areas of interest:

➤ employee characteristics (age, educational level, gender, family factors)

➤ employer/workplace characteristics (supervisory support, compensation, training, communication, co-worker support)

➤ client characteristics (age, disabilities, mental health, behavioural challenges, etc.).

Employee personal characteristics are largely outside of employer control. Therefore, our primary interest is the second group of variables (employer and workplace characteristics). Most of these factors can be influenced by managers and supervisors. Workplace factors, such as wages and benefits that cannot be completely "controlled" due to external circumstances such as funding, often can still be *influenced* with concerted effort over a period of years.

The latter focus (type of clients) is found exclusively in literature in the area of mental health, education, nursing, and rehabilitation (Poulin and Walter, 1992; Cooley and Yovanoff, 1996; Larson, Lakin and Bruininks, 1998; Weiss, 1999). Since most human service organizations are not able to choose their clientele, there is little employers can do to change how client demographics influence workplace quality, job satisfaction and retention.

It seems reasonable, therefore, to focus primarily on factors within our reach to change or influence rather than "givens" such as client/customer or employee characteristics.

Diagnosis versus Treatment

On balance, contemporary literature is heavily weighted on diagnosis of the problem of turnover rather than describing what can be done to improve the situation. While a few researchers focus on intervention strategies, the majority of contemporary articles and books analyze the *reasons* for turnover and low employee satisfaction.

For example, researchers found the following statistical correlations:

➟ turnover rates decrease as employee commitment to the organization increases

➟ turnover rates decrease as job satisfaction increases

➟ turnover rates decrease among employees who intend to stay in their jobs.

Not surprisingly, results show employees who are "committed" are more likely to intend to stay and employees who leave are less committed. (Armstrong, 1999; Spector, 2000).

There is a very strong possibility that commitment to the employer, intent to stay and also job satisfaction are different forms of one key variable. Speculatively, these variables are all *outcomes* and are indicators of workplace quality. In other words, people are more likely to stay if the environment is healthy, supportive, challenging, and educational. All of these factors would presumably support organizational commitment, create intent to stay and reduce turnover. Several meta-analyses have confirmed this observation (Spector, 2000).

There is a great deal of agreement among many researchers about employee and organizational factors that are correlated to decreased job satisfaction and increased turnover. Several key factors emerge repeatedly in dozens of research studies. It would seem reasonable to suggest these are the key factors defining the quality of a workplace. It would seem likely that employers who make improvements in these key areas will have more satisfied employees (Lauer and Gebhardt, 1997; Outlaw, 1998; Allen, Drevs and Ruhe, 1999).

The Retention Revolution

Before we turn to what the literature says about creating a quality workplace, one point bears mention. The past decade has witnessed an unprecedented shift toward the client/customer as king or queen. John Izzo and Pam Withers in *Values Shift, The New Work Ethic and What It Means for Business (Izzo and Withers, 2000)* describe the impact the exclusive focus on clients/customers has on employees. The customer service revolution caused many employees to encounter high expectations, long hours, ongoing critical feedback, minimal recognition, and rigid rules for doing things "right". These experiences have given many employees a clear indication they are, at best, second priority to their employers.

We appear to be at the vanguard of a *retention revolution* – where the *employee* is becoming queen or king. Theoretically, a satisfied employee (working in a quality workplace) is quite likely to:

➠ deliver excellent quality service to clients/customers

➠ be loyal to his/her employer

➠ be retained as an employee for years to come. (Buckingham and Coffman, 1999).

The values driving this revolution are seemingly the same as those that drove the customer service revolution. *If you want people to stay loyal (as clients/customers or employees), they must be treated well and feel the organization gives them very few reasons to consider going elsewhere.*

> **Good employees who leave must be understood to be organizational (rather than employee) failures.**

As is the case with customer service, it takes very little for an employee to become dissatisfied and a great deal of effort must be expended to ensure she or he is satisfied. McDonnell and Wilson-Simpson (1994) noted low pay seemed to be responsible for worker *dissatisfaction.* However, atmosphere, quality of supervision and autonomy were closely linked to *satisfaction* of employees.

It is no longer acceptable for employers to expect employees to work because they are paid an "honest day's wage". Across North America we are facing a cross-sector labour shortage which, by all accounts, will be long-term. This means skilled employees are at a premium. They will work where they are treated well and have a sense of belonging. (Sims and Veres, 1999; Izzo and Withers, 2000).

In the future, many organizations will find it necessary to provide on-the-job *basic skill development* for unskilled and lesser skilled employees. If these employees prove to be competent, motivated and trustworthy they are prime candidates for active recruitment by other employers. Employees will understand their skills are marketable. If their current working conditions are positive they will likely stay. If not, they will likely leave. The exit of these employees represents the loss of a significant investment in time and money spent on recruitment, orientation, training and supervision.

The Job Satisfaction Connection

Author Paul E. Spector (2000) reported 12,400 studies on job satisfaction were published in the psychological literature between 1972 and 1991. Many of these studies established that job satisfaction is connected to factors relating to the atmosphere at work (the climate experienced by employees) and to turnover rates (the outcome of the workplace climate).

Rather than relate the detailed findings of specific studies, we will capture and discuss the factors repeatedly found to be related to job satisfaction. A complete listing of the studies reviewed is included in the Reference section at the end of this book.

The following chart lists (in no particular order) the organizational factors that academic researchers and various book authors have correlated with job satisfaction.

Human Factors	Environmental Factors
◆ Quality supervision (support, feedback, communication)	◆ Input into decisions that affect the employee
◆ Co-worker support	◆ Scope of work and job variety
◆ Fair treatment	◆ Fair/competitive wages and benefits
◆ Assistance when mistakes are made	◆ Safety
◆ Support when personal problems arise	◆ Having the materials, equipment and technology needed
◆ Co-workers who care about doing a good job	◆ Hours of work (schedule)
◆ Inspiring leadership	◆ Flexible hours
◆ Doing work that makes a difference and helps others	◆ Training and career development opportunities
◆ Frequent people contact	◆ Meaningful performance appraisals
◆ Mentoring and coaching	◆ Clarity of duties and expectations
◆ Teamwork	◆ Time away from work for family and personal lives

Human Factors	Environmental Factors
◆ Communication	◆ Recognition, rewards and acknowledgement
◆ Meaningful, positive feedback	◆ Job security
◆ A sense of belonging and friendship	◆ Autonomy and independence
◆ Properly managed critical feedback and discipline	◆ Opportunity to learn new skills and be challenged

It should be noted, studies have divergent findings on the *relative importance* of many of these factors. For example, some studies found that wages and benefits were the most important factor in determining job satisfaction and turnover (McDonnell and Wilson-Simpson, 1994; VRRI, 2000). Others found that wages were of lesser importance (Lauer and Gebhardt, 1997). Still others noted that some managers felt wages were more important to employees than the employees themselves did (Herman, 1999). Finally, there appears to be a tendency for managers to emphasize external problems beyond their control rather than internal factors within their influence, as causes for job dissatisfaction and turnover (Blankertz and Robinson, 1997).

Job satisfaction studies have defined and measured variables (primarily employer/workplace factors) which managers can change or at least influence. This makes it possible for an organization to determine specifically what issues need to be addressed and what areas of the operation are strong suits. To gather information from employees, managers must carefully craft surveys that accurately measure employees' opinions on various aspects of the organization's functioning (Outlaw, 1998; Allen, Drevs and Ruhe, 1999; Daniels, 1999; Kaye and Jordan-Evans, 1999). In fact, *job satisfaction* is a bit of a misnomer. More accurately, surveys measure employees' satisfaction with the workplace *as a whole* – not just with employees' specific job duties.

Since employee satisfaction has been found to be a precursor to retention, we *may* be able to predict future turnover or retention by first measuring satisfaction. Because employee satisfaction is a multi-dimensional construct, results from satisfaction surveys can point the way for managers and supervisors to improve the quality of the workplace.

Specific Findings Related to Satisfaction & Employee Characteristics

Several studies on job satisfaction provide some interesting observations with respect to certain employee characteristics.

1. Job satisfaction was found to be higher among older employees (many of whom also had longer tenure with their employer), and for employees who had lesser educational qualifications (Blankertz and Robinson, 1997; Spector, 2000).

2. Dissatisfied employees have increased frequency of physical complaints (e.g. sleep disruptions and gastro-intestinal symptoms) increased absenteeism and increased reports of anxiety and depression (Spector, 2000).

3.   Short-term employees (six months and less) appear to have significantly higher turnover rates. Lauer and Gebhardt (1997) reported that half of the turnover experienced by organizations occurred in the first thirty days of employment. Employees with longer tenure are more likely to remain with their current employer.

The Compensation Connection

Many studies have investigated the relationship between compensation (wages or salary, and benefits), job satisfaction and turnover.   The link seems obvious – better paid employees are more likely to remain with their employer. However, two other factors emerge. First, authors have noted that employees in some workplaces value other organizational factors over their level of compensation (Levesque, 1996; Taunton et al, 1997; Allan, Crevs and Ruhe, 1999). Secondly, internal workplace equity in how wages are set for different employees appears to be more important than actual pay levels for some employees (Spector, 2000). Blankertz and Robinson (1997) found that mental health workers were most likely to resign as a result of stress and burnout. Compensation level was a secondary factor contributing to resignations.

McDonnell and Wilson-Simpson (1994) noted that since salary levels are likely to remain low for some time to come, efforts to improve the quality of the workplace are the most efficient way to retain employees.

The relationship between low compensation and turnover was described by both employees and supervisors in the Larsen et al (1998) study of residential agencies serving people with disabilities. They reported that low wages had impact on both turnover (increasing it) and recruitment, making it more difficult to hire qualified new staff. Roberts and Sarvela (1990) found that pay and benefits were the leading cause of home care workers leaving their jobs.

A recent study in Alberta (VRRI, 2000) found turnover and wage levels appear to be closely correlated in the rehabilitation field. This study also found that different types of work (e.g. residential vs. vocational), size of community, organizational size, and geographic location are also related to different levels of turnover.

Managers frequently report that wages and benefits play a major role in being able to recruit and retain employees (Blankertz and Robinson, 1997; Herman, 1999; VRRI, 2000). However, there is some evidence to suggest that managers actually over-estimate the role played by wages in this picture (Herman, 1999; Kaye and Jordan-Evans, 1999). Lauer and Gebhardt (1997) maintain the most common reason for employee resignations was lack of recognition and praise, not low wages and benefits, as many managers believe. Blankertz and Robinson (1997) found that employees said job stress and burnout were the most frequent reasons for resigning. However, managers in the same organizations reported most employees resigned to pursue opportunities elsewhere, to return to school or because of poor wages.

Finally, Levesque (1996) pointed out that competitive pay and benefits ranked fifth as a reason for employee resignations behind other factors such as inflexible policies, authoritarian managers or supervisors, poor organization of work, and lack of direction. Factors identified by employees as less important than pay and benefits were:

➠ lack of recognition

➠ lack of incentives

➠ unsafe/unhealthy working conditions

➠ difficult co-worker relationships

➠ skill of supervisors and managers.

The prevailing belief that poor compensation is *primarily* responsible for turnover may be discouraging managers and supervisors from working to improve other very important workplace quality issues. Compensation is *an issue* but not necessarily *the primary issue* from the perspective of employees in many organizations.

The Part-Time Connection

Unfortunately, the Alberta study (VRRI, 2000) did not separate employees who worked part-time from full-time employees. Part-timers usually have lower annual incomes. Rather than being solely or primarily a reflection of low annual income, these higher turnover rates among part-time employees could reflect a variety of organization factors.

This perspective is supported by Levesque (1996) who noted that part-time employee turnover was related to (in descending order of importance):

➠ lesser status of part-time compared to other employees

➠ less attention from supervisors

➠ being assigned more undesirable tasks

➠ less job security

➠ lower incomes

➠ fewer benefits

➠ varied, unreliable and/or irregular hours.

The Recognition Connection

Employees also need recognition and rewards in order to be satisfied with their employment situations. Behavioural psychology has clearly determined individuals value different types and frequencies of recognition or rewards. Recognition is symbolic – intended to show appreciation for accomplishments or contributions. Rewards are tangible and are intended to positively influence future performance (Sims and Veres, 1999).

Human relations literature and practices widely recognizes the importance of positive feedback in various forms. Much attention has been paid to the ineffectiveness of traditional recognition and reward programs used by employers. Traditional approaches fall short of their goal because the feedback:

⟹ is too general; it is often not clear what behaviours, standards, or achievements are being recognized

⟹ often rewards average performers rather than employees who are excellent performers

⟹ is focused on mid-term and long-term employees who are *least* likely to leave

⟹ does not give the employee anything of real or lasting value (e.g. trinkets rather than further training, new challenges, etc.)

⟹ reflects what the organization is prepared to give rather than what individual employees need or want

⟹ is often discretionary (granted subjectively by supervisors or managers) or arbitrary, not allowing for clear understanding why certain employees receive recognition and others do not

⟹ creates divisions among employees who must then work together

⟹ is often delayed by several months, lessening the impact of the feedback even if it is valued by the employee (Daniels, 1999).

Associated with rewards and recognition, incentives are intended to increase performance and are often specific to certain goals or targets. Incentives must be earned. Employees know in advance what they must to do for the incentive to be made available.

To be effective incentives must:

➠ be understood to exist before the employee begins a task or project

➠ be available to employees who are capable of improving their performance

➠ be valued or wanted by the employee

➠ be achievable with reasonable effort

➠ have few barriers or constraints in order to be earned

➠ be delivered immediately and frequently (Daniels, 1999).

The Gender and Family Connection

Although there are a limited number of studies on the subject of gender and turnover, some studies have found turnover to be higher among women who are raising young children. Glass and Riley (1998) found that mothers of pre-schoolers change jobs more often than non-mothers or mothers of older children. They also noted increased frequency of job change resulted in generally lower wages and women occupying less prestigious positions than those who remained in positions longer. Most mothers of newborns who intended to return to work after maternity leave, in fact did return (72 percent). However, within a year after birth, 12 percent had left the workforce and 21 percent had changed jobs.

Causes of job-family conflict were found to be:

- ⮚ frequent or required overtime hours
- ⮚ high workloads and demanding work
- ⮚ afternoon shifts
- ⮚ unsupportive supervisors
- ⮚ health and safety issues on the job site
- ⮚ lack of reliable, quality childcare.

There is a tendency for supervisors or managers to see women's decisions to resign after childbirth as reflecting family, home or personal factors rather than workplace conditions and policies. Underlying this is a belief that child bearing and child raising are incompatible with continuous employment. Work disruption and resignations after childbirth are regarded as normal and unavoidable. As a result, some employers fail to make appropriate adjustments (e.g. increased social support, flexibility of working hours, policy changes and allowing sick leave to be used to care for children) that would likely improve retention of new mothers.

Women who remained employed after childbirth were more likely to:

- ⮚ have had longer maternity leaves
- ⮚ work with other women who have preschool aged children
- ⮚ have interesting work
- ⮚ work evening shifts

- have flexible working hours

- have higher levels of workplace and co-worker support

- have better education

- have longer tenures

- be paid higher wages

- have partners who earned lower incomes. (Glass and Riley, 1998).

The Recruitment Connection

Dibble (1999) noted that retention of qualified employees actually begins with:

- having clear up-to-date job descriptions

- a good recruitment and selection process

- effective new employee orientation programs.

Employees who have talents and skills that match the requirements of their jobs are more likely to be satisfied with their work and therefore, more likely to stay in their jobs longer (Levesque, 1996; Blankertz and Robinson, 1997; Buckingham and Coffman, 1999).

Employee dismissals during the probationary period and dismissals after completion of probation can result in 10 to 15 percent turnover per year (Larson, Lakin and Bruininks, 1998; VRRI, 2000). Levesque (1996) noted that reasons for probationary employee dismissals were primarily employer (rather than employee) related. The reasons most often cited were:

- ⮞ poor screening practices
- ⮞ no pre-employment measures of actual job skills
- ⮞ interviews that were not specific to the job or skills required
- ⮞ absent or weak orientation program
- ⮞ supervisors who paid insufficient attention to new employees.

Spector (2000) states that employees who liked (or disliked) their previous job were much more apt to like (or dislike) their next job. Since job satisfaction connects to turnover rates, hiring employees who liked their previous work should have a positive impact on employee retention.

The work of the Gallup Organization described in *First Break All the Rules,* (Marcus Buckingham and Curt Coffman, 1999) is ground-breaking in identifying the importance of matching employee talents, which are not acquired and cannot be learned, with their positions. Supervisors and managers can reasonably be expected to teach, train and coach employees to build the skills necessary to be successful in their jobs. However, some employees are placed in positions (at initial recruitment, through internal reassignment or via promotions) which do not match their true talents. If an employee is expected to excel at tasks that she or he cannot (because the tasks are non-talents for the employee) then she or he has been miscast. Casting for talent is a key factor in creating satisfied employees. Well-cast employees are much more likely to be retained. Miscast employees may also be excellent in *other jobs* that are better aligned with their talents. It is the employer's responsibility to ensure miscast employees are given the opportunity to use their true talents in other roles (Buckingham and Coffman, 1999).

A recruitment related issue is that employers with high turnover rates may also have greater difficulty recruiting new employees. The same workplace conditions that influence people's decisions to leave seem to discourage others from applying (Kaye and Jordan-Evans, 1999).

Added to this is that the workforce size is declining. Izzo and Withers (1999) and Larsen et al (1998) note that the number of available skilled workers is declining globally and across virtually all sectors. This is not a temporary state of affairs as some employers believe. There is in fact, a clear demographic shift in the workforce. Baby-boomers are aging and many are retiring before age 65. There are fewer potential employees in Generation X, and the so-called Nintendo Generation. These employees are less willing to work two jobs, or long overtime hours in one job in order to make ends meet. This highlights the importance of employers building strategies to keep the quality employees they already have. The fastest way to solve the recruitment problem is to recruit significantly fewer people in the years ahead.

The Generational Connection

In their recent book, *Values Shift: The New Work Ethic and What It Means for Business (2000)*, management consultants and authors John Izzo and Pam Withers detail six expectations of employees in the new workforce. These include:

➠ the expectation of balance and synergy

➠ the expectation of work as a noble cause

➠ the expectation of personal growth and development

➠ the expectation of partnership

➠ the expectation of community at work

➠ the expectation of trust.

Supporting their theses with a myriad of well-documented research (academic, demographic and socio-cultural) the authors make a very strong case for a kinder, gentler workplace in the future. To a significant degree, the demand for change in workplace quality is being driven by a younger workforce with different values than their parents and their baby boomer supervisors and managers. These "new" employees are the supervisors and managers of the future. Major organizational workplace quality shifts are simply a matter of time.

Present-day managers would be wise to integrate workplace improvements into annual operational planning and human resource practices. Put simply, the current cross-sector international labour shortage increasingly puts the employee of the future in the driver's seat. Employers must learn to create quality workplaces that are a good fit with the new generation of employees' needs and values.

Long hours with little time for personal lives or family will be unacceptable to employees. Work is not just a place to earn a living, it is a place where meaningful relationships and a sense of belonging must exist. Opportunities to work for the good of society, not just for the good of the "mother corp." are crucial for employee satisfaction and retention in the future (Izzo and Withers, 2000).

Painting Your Current Turnover Picture

Chapter 3

High employee turnover is discouraging for managers and supervisors. Since you are reading this book, you are likely curious about what can be done to tame turnover in your organization or team. You may even be absolutely sure you can make things better for you, your employees and your clients/customers.

"Accept things as they are, not as you wish them to be."

Napoleon

To take the next steps, you must be prepared to see things as they are. To see your turnover picture, you need to gather accurate historical and current information.

The first step on the journey to improving employee retention is determining what current turnover rates are. This requires you to:

➠ create a working definition of avoidable turnover

➠ accurately assess turnover rates for the past one to three years

➠ carefully analyze the turnover information

➠ develop a plan targeting areas with highest turnover.

41

How Big is Your Challenge?

There are two possible approaches to measuring turnover and setting targets for improved retention of employees. The simplest approach is to measure turnover for the organization as a whole. Using this approach, you would count all employees who leave the organization for any reason and then calculate what percentage of your total workforce this represents. You could also repeat this process for each department, area or program in the organization. Finally, you would decide what your targeted percentage is for reducing turnover.

While simple, this approach has several limitations. First, by including all positions vacated you will artificially inflate your turnover picture. Consider the number of seasonal, contract, temporary, retiring and on-leave employees who would be counted in this figure. Next, think about how you would determine your retention target. You would have to guesstimate and could set an unrealistic expectation for your organization or for specific supervisors and managers.

The solution to these problems is to carefully separate avoidable and unavoidable turnover. You will then be able to set a realistic target for improving retention.

Developing a Turnover Definition

There is no one correct definition of turnover – so you must develop a definition that works for your organization. Here are the four steps to create your working definition.

Step 1: Separate avoidable turnover from unavoidable turnover in your definition. Your goal is to target turnover that can be changed (i.e. avoidable turnover). Examples of *un*avoidable turnover include:

> *"That which gets measured, gets done."*
>
> Unknown

➠ planned retirement

➠ family relocation (e.g. related to spouse/partner being transferred

➠ serious injuries or disability which does not permit the employee to be retrained for other work in the organization

➠ physical and mental illnesses that are progressive and/or uncontrolled by medication or other therapies

➠ seasonal (e.g. summer students), contract or temporary employees who leave after a certain period of time.

Be careful not to add items to your list that are *avoidable*. For example, most employees who return to school, do so by choice. Your organization or department may be able to support school and part-time work and/or educational leave, which encourages the employee to remain part of your workforce. Some employees may actually delay schooling because they enjoy their work so much.

43

Step 2: Identify what *positions* will be excluded when calculating your turnover rates. Excluded positions may include:

⟫ those that are contracted from time to time to cover high work volumes

⟫ summer or seasonal temporary positions

⟫ positions that were closed due to downsizing or restructuring with resulting layoffs of employees.

Again, care should be taken not to exclude too many positions in an effort to minimize your turnover rates. The goal is to capture your organization's or department's situation *as it really is.*

Step 3: Determine how far back in time you will gather turnover information. Factors to consider are:

⟫ How far back can payroll or personnel records be easily accessed? Ideally you would like three years of historical information.

⟫ Were there major organizational changes in a particular year that may have caused turnover to change dramatically? For example, layoffs due to financial hardship or restructuring should be factored out of your analysis.

⟫ Events can change your turnover picture, including: manager or supervisor changes, significant changes to wages or benefits or payment of bonuses. The timing of these types of changes should be carefully noted for use later in your analysis.

Step 4: Decide how your turnover information will be grouped. This is crucial for understanding and later targeting specific areas of the organization experiencing higher turnover. You should consider each of the following groupings for your data:

⟩⟩▶ turnover by department, site, program or geographic area

⟩⟩▶ turnover for each supervisor's and/or manager's areas of responsibility

⟩⟩▶ turnover for full-time and part-time positions

⟩⟩▶ turnover for night and weekend positions

⟩⟩▶ turnover for relief or casual positions

⟩⟩▶ turnover in specific positions considered to be high stress or demanding

⟩⟩▶ turnover for positions that are in isolated locations, where employees work primarily alone or travel

⟩⟩▶ turnover for employees with less than three (or six) months of service with the organization

⟩⟩▶ turnover among longer service employees (e.g. 3-5 years, 5-10 years, etc.)

⟩⟩▶ turnover among employees with certain educational qualifications or levels of training

- ➠ turnover among employees returning from maternity leave

- ➠ turnover among specific age groups

- ➠ turnover among women and among men

- ➠ turnover among employees consistently working more than normal full-time hours

- ➠ turnover among employees who work unusual or extended shifts (e.g. 48-hour weekends, 12-hour days, 6 or more days of continuous work)

- ➠ turnover among employees who are on-call during "off hours".

Remember that the more groupings you choose, the more work you create when summarizing and analyzing the information. Choose groupings that seem particularly relevant or that may point to areas you already suspect are turnover "hot spots".

Measuring Avoidable Turnover

Now that you have your definition, it's time to gather some information. Here are the next steps to follow.

Step 1: Gather the information using the following general formula:

Total number of employee exits for **all** positions
for a one year period

minus

The number of employee exits that were *unavoidable*
(retirement, students, etc.)

minus

The number of employee exits for excluded positions

equals

The number of employee exits which were *avoidable.*

Divide this number by

The total **average** number of employees in the organization
during the year (see formula on the next page)

multiplied by 100
equals

The annual avoidable turnover.

The average number of employees during a year is calculated using the following formula:

Number of employees at the beginning of the year

plus

Number of employees at the end of the year

divided by 2

When you begin to gather information, be prepared for a few cracks to appear in your turnover definition. Make reasonable adjustments to your definition (e.g. add or delete certain positions) to create the most realistic picture possible.

Ensure the information collected can be grouped as you decided in Step 4 of the previous section.

Step 2: Prepare a brief summary report that identifies:

⮞ turnover for the whole organization for each year

⮞ turnover by department, area, worksite, manager or supervisor, etc.

⮞ turnover for the various groupings you identified in Step 4 in the previous section.

Clearly mark the times when major organizational changes occurred which might influence your turnover data.

A Picture is Worth a Thousand Words

It is helpful to show these data using a series of graphs or charts. This creates a picture of turnover in your organization that will be very useful for future comparison. It also enables you to share your information easily with employees, stakeholders, funders, and the board of directors. Charting your data over a period of several years will clearly indicate the success of your retention strategies in the long term. Charts and graphs will also help you flag areas of the organization needing further attention.

Analyzing Your Turnover Picture

You may be feeling a bit daunted or perhaps even overwhelmed by the volume of information you have assembled. Your next challenge is to make sense of it all so you can:

➠ identify particular areas of concern

➠ set priorities for action among these areas

➠ target areas where turnover is highest with specific retention strategies.

Information is power but only when you act on what you know.

Don't get discouraged with "how bad" certain areas look. Remember you can and will improve employee retention – but first you must be prepared to see and acknowledge things as they really are.

49

You will likely find some areas of the organization have better retention than other areas. This is certainly reason to celebrate! Understanding what is going on in these areas (i.e. what is causing them to have better than average retention) will also give you some ideas about what you can do to improve the situation in higher turnover areas.

Step 1: Look for areas (positions, sites, teams, etc.) that have significantly *below average* turnover and ask, "WHY?" Answering this question may require you to speculate, discuss possible reasons with others and ask the employees who work in the areas with lower turnover why they think retention is better than in other areas, programs or positions.

> *"The same old analysis leads to paralysis."*
>
> Unknown

Be careful to resist overly simple or superficial explanations. For example, it may appear that retention is good because all the positions are full-time with benefits. Other factors such as flexibility, autonomy, involvement in decision-making and opportunities to learn may be equally viable explanations for better retention rates.

Step 2: Look for areas (positions, sites, teams, etc.) with *above average* turnover and ask, "WHY?" Again you may need to "guess" and then gather information to check out your interpretations.

Step 3: As part of your analysis, you may wish to ask employees why they stay, what's going well and what could be improved. This can be done in the form of:

➠ an anonymous survey of all or some employees

➠ in-person or telephone interviews

➠ discussion groups with employees clustered by site, supervisor, job duties or client/customer demographics.

Satisfaction surveys are discussed fully in Chapter 7.

Estimating Turnover Costs Your Organization

You may be satisfied just knowing what your turnover or retention picture looks like. However, some managers may want to estimate the actual cost saving available when retention is improved. Estimating the cost of current *avoidable* turnover can also help identify the budget available for increased retention efforts. There is nothing more compelling to a senior manager who may be unsure of the value of creating a retention program as demonstrating the effect decreasing turnover will have on the bottom line.

> *"Adversity reveals genius and prosperity conceals it."*
>
> Horace

In order to estimate turnover costs, answer the following list of questions as accurately as possible. You may need to involve accountants, managers, supervisors and human resources personnel to get estimates or actual figures for some questions. It is recommended you estimate the costs based on a single employee as your unit of measurement. Even though you may recruit more than one person from each competition or advertisement, you will find the math easier if you adjust these figures to reflect a single position.

Turnover Cost Calculation Worksheet

		# of hours x $ per hour	$ cost
1.	Time spent discussing resignation and planning the hiring process		
2.	Time spent preparing ad(s), flyers, postings, etc.		
3.	Time spent distributing flyers, postings and placing ad(s)		
4.	Cost of running ad(s)		
5.	Initial review/screening of applicants		
6.	Responding to telephone & e-mail inquiries		
7.	Time spent contacting applicants & scheduling interviews		
8.	Time spent preparing for interviews (resume reviews, coordinating interview team, preparing questions, etc.		
9.	Time spent interviewing by interview team		
10.	Time spent discussing best candidate		
11.	Time spent checking references		
12.	Time spent completing other checks		

		# of hours x $ per hour	$ cost
	(security, criminal record, etc.)		
13.	Time spent making job offer, preparing offer letter, confirming acceptance		
14.	Cost of coverage, relief and overtime to fill shifts or job duties of vacant position		
15.	Initial orientation by managers & supervisors, payroll & personnel		
16.	Orientation by co-workers (including job duties, tours, meetings with clients/customers, etc.)		
17.	Cost of double staffing during orientation/training		
18.	Cost of employee time for basic training (courses, workshops, etc.)		
	Fees to attend		
19.	Other costs		
20.	Other costs		

Setting Retention Targets

If prepared carefully, your turnover picture will let you set specific and realistic targets for improved retention for individual departments, supervisory groupings, areas or teams. You may also wish to establish retention targets for the organization as a whole. For example:

Target Area	Current Retention Rate	Targeted Retention Rate
Department A	65%	72%
Department B	72%	77%
Team 1	43%	60%
Team 2	69%	74%
Relief & Casual	42%	62%
Whole Organization	76%	81%

Decisions about reasonable targets should be made with the input of employees and supervisors. Reasons for past years' turnover should be taken into account, as should the groups' ability to create the necessary changes.

We always go where we are looking.

It is also wise to set multi-year (three to five year) targets. The greatest improvements in retention are often possible in the first year or two. Target larger percentage improvements in these two years and smaller improvements in subsequent years.

Now the real work begins. Chapters 4 through 7 describe 55 strategies that will ensure you successfully meet your retention targets.

Part 2

Transforming What We Know into What We Do –

55 Strategies for Improving Retention

*"Whatever you can do,
or dream you can, begin it.
Boldness has genius,
power and magic in it."*

Goethe

Begin at the Beginning – Recruitment and Selection

Chapter 4

There are really three issues surrounding recruitment. First, you need to find quality candidates to interview and it seems they are increasingly in short supply. Second, the research suggests that one-third to one-half of annual turnover is comprised of employees who are dismissed. Third, as much as half the employees that some organizations lose during a year leave during the first three months. The latter two factors point to problems with recruitment and also with orientation (please see Chapter 5).

Improving recruitment, selection and orientation practices is at the heart of any retention initiative. If you do it right the first time you won't have to fix it.

I have heard many managers and supervisors lament, "There are just no qualified applicants anymore." They are commenting on the small number of people responding to advertisements placed in local papers. These ads once generated dozens and sometimes hundreds of applications. While we complained about having to screen and interview so many people, most managers would like to go back to "the good old days" even for just one competition!

What has also changed are the qualifications of applicants. Once employers had a pool of qualified people from which to choose. Now the pool is a mere puddle and seems to be continuing to shrink.

Perhaps we need to reframe this dilemma. First, consider the idea that the best people, those who we wished were working for us, are working somewhere else. Rather than believing "the good people are no longer out there", we need to create ways of letting people know we need them to work for *us*. This means we need to change our strategies in order to find and attract them. Small conventional newspaper ads are not likely to have any impact because most of these people are not looking for jobs.

Secondly, we need to rethink "qualified" as "quality". We can train for skill but not for talent or for attitude. Perhaps our practices must shift to hiring people who have talents, values and qualities that match our organization's needs. Then we must orient, train and supervise so they gain competence and confidence in their job tasks. Unlike the employees of the past who came "ready-made" to our qualification specifications, employees of the future will be "custom-fitted" by us. Hiring for talent, values and attitude is therefore, essential. Most everything else can be learned.

There are dozens of books and book chapters devoted to the technical steps of proper recruitment (please refer to "There's More to Read" at the end of this chapter). You may also wish to read my earlier book *The Supervisor's Big Book of Answers*

(1999). Consulting these resources is essential as you develop your recruitment policies and practices. Make sure you choose books that are less than five years old. Human resource theory and practice changes over time and you want to use only current ideas in developing your recruitment guidelines.

The following series of strategies are not intended to cover the basics of recruitment. Instead, these ideas are intended to spark some creative approaches to attracting, screening, interviewing and selecting employees. Recruitment is an active (go find 'em) rather than a passive (let 'em come to us) process.

> *"Doing the same thing over and over will never give you a different result."*
>
> Unknown

The tried and tired practice of placing advertisements in the newspaper is no longer generating the kind of response that justifies the expense. The following 20 strategies will help you explore some new options.

Strategy #1 Look in different places for applicants

Consider posting advertisements or organizational newsletters in locations where likely candidates may be found. Possibilities include:

➠ churches and church bulletins

➠ laundromats

➠ shopping centres

➠ pharmacies, grocery stores and banks

➠ professional offices (doctors, dentists, chiropractors, etc.)

- sports centres (arenas, bowling alleys, swimming pools)
- neighborhood or community newsletters
- daycares and schools
- college and university student housing
- college and university newspapers.

To customize this list for your organization and community, hold a brainstorming session with current employees and clients/customers. Make sure you record where you place your ads or flyers and ask applicants where they saw your job posting. Track which locations have the best response and don't return to those that generate little or no interest.

Strategy #2 Look further afield

Across the country there are areas with high unemployment and underemployment. Underemployment means that there are people with qualifications that are greater than required by the positions they are holding. This means you should consider recruiting (or at least advertising) in areas beyond your own community. For example, a few organizations in Alberta, where there is a serious labour shortage, have been successful in hiring people from the Maritimes and Newfoundland, where unfortunately unemployment is the highest in Canada.

The excessive cost of interviewing in person may be avoided by using telephone screening, multiple telephone interviews and comprehensive reference checks. If you have access to internet technology and a camera – a "virtual interview" video conference is very inexpensive.

Within your community, especially in urban centres, there may also be immigrants or new Canadians who are looking for work. If English is their second language, they may experience real difficulty finding jobs that match their educational or experiential qualifications. Approaching cultural organizations, service clubs or sponsoring agencies (such as churches) may lead to some successful recruitment possibilities.

Strategy #3   Ask current employees for referrals

Your current employees should be an endless supply of connections and referrals for new employees. Happy employees are great ambassadors for employers. Don't overlook their family members and friends as contacts as well.

Researchers have found retention rates are higher among new employees referred by current employees. This could be because current employees fill the new person in on exactly what to expect on the job and from the organization. Consider creating an incentive for employees by using a "finder's fee" for each applicant referred and a higher fee if the person is offered a position and accepts. The "fee" may be:

➠ a cash incentive

➠ a point system toward special benefits or larger items (this encourages ongoing referrals)

➣ additional training opportunities

➣ prizes or special gifts (these must have real value to employees – avoid mugs, pens and T-shirts)

➣ additional benefits (e.g. holiday time, bonus days)

➣ coupons or discounts for local businesses (e.g. free winter car inspection or tire rotation)

➣ lottery or fundraising tickets.

Consult your employees about what they would like to see on the list. Offering a range of incentives will be better than offering just one or two. What appeals to one person may not appeal to others. For overly zealous employees, you may need to set a limit on the number of incentive payments available in any one year.

Strategy #4 Attend public events and community functions to network and recruit

Count the number of special events, group dinners and public gatherings you have attended in the past year or so. Multiply this by the number of colleagues or co-workers with whom you work. Together you have contact with hundreds, perhaps thousands of people in a year. Use these opportunities to network with people who may be potential candidates or may know someone who is looking for a new challenge.

Always carry a few basic recruitment supplies to these types of gatherings including:

➠ your business cards and/or cards for the person who does the hiring in your organization

➠ a brochure about the organization

➠ a flyer or job posting sheet.

If someone seems interested or has a potential referral, always follow up with them by telephone or e-mail a few days later.

Volunteering for community-based organizations (e.g. sitting on boards or committees) is another way to network.

Strategy #5 Treat recruitment as an ongoing, rather than position-specific activity

Our current economy is driving organizational growth at unprecedented rates. Gone are the days when organizations are fully staffed. Growth and turnover create the need for constant recruitment. Make your recruitment strategies broad-based and long term. Use many different approaches with many involved people at the same time. Keep careful records of what approaches are resulting in the best number of responses. Keep generating new approaches. Try at least one new approach every two or three months.

Strategy #6 Host open houses, special community events and job fairs

The intent of these events is to draw a wide range of community members into your organization's facilities or programs. Once they have arrived, educate them about what you do and let them know you are looking for motivated, talented and skilled people. This is part of teaching the broader community your organization is "open for business" in more than one way. People may or may not know what you really "do over there". Bring them through your door and you have a chance to educate *and* attract new talent.

Strategy #7 Create your own internal headhunter program

When you visit other organizations or businesses, look for employees who seem to be customer service oriented, pleasant, are good communicators, efficient and/or are skilled in areas similar to your work. Approach these people saying: "You know, you have a really great way with people. My organization is always looking for new people who have something positive to contribute. If you're ever interested, here's how you can reach us."

The risk of using this strategy is that you may end up recruiting under-qualified people. However, many employers have discovered the value of hiring for attitude and training for skills. A second risk is that you may not be very popular with other employers from whom you recruit staff. However, if these employers have really great workplaces – their employees will not be tempted to leave no matter who approaches them.

Strategy #8 Develop a partnership with local high schools for volunteer and/or work placement programs

Historically, high schools have approached employers about volunteer work or work placement experiences for students. Why not approach local high school principals, individually or as a group, and propose a partnership program? The program could include:

➠ students volunteering part of their school day or after school

➠ students working part-time (or relief or casual) when their age and academic standing allows

➠ students completing work placements with the organization.

One employer has created just such a partnership. When a student volunteer turns 18 years of age, he/she is presented with a birthday card and an offer of part-time employment with the organization.   In their volunteer roles, students have received basic training (e.g. first aid, CPR, crisis intervention, orientation to policies, etc.). They are actually better qualified than many candidates who respond to job advertisements.

Strategy #9   Develop a recruitment package and video

A recruitment package should include:

➠ general organizational information (history, size, structure, client/customer profiles, legal status)

➠ position descriptions (or sample job descriptions)

➠ brochures or other promotional information

➠ business cards of key people involved in hiring (human resources manager, supervisors, or senior manager)

➠ information about how to apply for positions and how to get additional information

➠ clearly stated reasons why someone should consider working for your organization (e.g. employee testimonials, pictures of teams working together, how his/her work will make a difference, benefits, training available, etc.).

Make this package available to anyone who inquires, responds to advertisements, to all current employees and at all organizational events.

Many organizations have created general information or public relations videos. With a little extra work and money, these videos can be edited to become a specific recruitment tool. The video should depict employees doing real jobs and speaking about why they choose to work with your organization. Keep it short, upbeat and informative. Make multiple copies and lend the video to anyone who would like to use it.

Strategy #10   When you advertise - be creative!

Many job ads run in newspapers may as well say:

> "Boring, low paid job available. Long hours, no benefits, lousy boss. Please apply to …"

To create better ads, hold a series of brainstorming sessions with current employees about what attracts them to their work and to the organization. Create a master list entitled "Our Best Stuff" and include one or two of these ideas in every ad you run.   Make good use of catchy first phrases.   One organization's advertisements start with:

> "The toughest job you'll ever learn to love."

Look at ads run by other organizations. Analyze what makes some appealing and others routine. You could also try placing ads in sections other than the employment section. Recently, a local newspaper made and error and ran a small employment advertisement in the "Community Notices" section of the paper. The organization received three times their usual number of replies to ads placed in the classified section. Well written "news articles" about your services, clients/customers in local newspapers can also draw attention from people who may be looking for a new challenge.

Carefully track the response rates for different ads and different placements. In addition, you may find it valuable to analyze the quality of the applicants who respond to various ads.

Strategy #11 Maximize use of technology for getting the word out

If you don't yet have your own website you may want to consider creating one. Make sure you include up-to-date information about positions available, closing dates and how to apply. Include video clips illustrating the type of job duties and/or audio clips from current employees about why this is a great place to work.

Trying to operate without a website in the new millenium is like trying to operate without a telephone in the 1970s.

There are an ever-increasing number of websites acting as information clearinghouses for people looking for new jobs and employers with openings. A list of these is included in Appendix 1. Consider posting vacant positions with one or more of these services.

Strategy #12 Speed-up your recruitment process

As a result of using these new recruitment strategies, the number of people applying for positions will most certainly increase. Now the challenge is to hire them before someone else does.

Many candidates report waiting weeks or even months for a response from prospective employers. This does not speak well of the organization's efficiency, care for people or personnel practices. The best candidates will have accepted positions elsewhere if your response time is too slow.

Tips for shortening recruitment time include:

➠ Before you post a position, create your interview team, set your interview dates and times. Delays are often caused by trying to juggle 2 or 3 busy people's schedules.

Your goal is to be service-oriented during all phases of the recruitment process.

➠ If you do not have a human resources manager, designate one employee to be responsible for receiving and acknowledging all applications.

➠ Screen applications as they arrive; this rewards the early birds who may also be the most energetic and motivated new employees. Contact suitable candidates immediately to set up an interview.

➠ Have two people screen applications; if necessary have both quickly re-screen all applications to create your short list.

➠ Complete screening interviews by telephone to shorten the list of in-person interviews required.

➠ If there are delays, contact candidates who will be interviewed and let them know what's happening. Ask particularly attractive candidates to not accept another position without calling you first.

➤ Complete reference checks only on candidates who are being seriously considered for a job offer. Using reference checks as a screening tool is a big time waster.

➤ Make your decision hours, not days, after your interviews are complete.

➤ Make the job offer immediately after making the decision; you can make the offer conditional on completing other background (e.g. criminal record) checks.

<u>Strategy #13</u>   Create realistic job previews

Research has shown that systematic use of realistic job previews substantially reduced turnover in some settings. The intent of job previews is to increase the understanding by prospective new employees of job duties and working conditions. The goal is to present a non-distorted view of the job, the organization and clients/customers.

A job preview may include:

➤ information provided by current employees who are doing the same or similar job

➤ real life home videos (i.e. non-professional) of a day-in-the-life on the job

➤ partial or full preview shifts/workday guided by a current staff or supervisor

➤ written information (e.g. question and answer sheets)

➠ specific information addressing things an employee must know or may have unrealistic expectations about (e.g. flexibility of working hours, travel required, team composition, level of autonomy).

Strategy #14   Screen for quality, not just for qualifications

Quality people are those who are a good match for your organization's values and have the attitudes, gifts or talents you desire. Resume information is focused on skills, experience and education (i.e. the applicant's qualifications). The

> *"If you refuse to accept anything but the best, you very often get it."*
> Somerset Maugham

quality of applicants, therefore, may not be obvious. As a result, short screening interviews (by telephone for efficiency or in-person if necessary) may be needed. A written assessment may also be valuable. Either way, your intent is to broaden your understanding of qualities of the applicant in addition to their skills.

Questions should focus on key elements of the position that are less related to skill and more related to attitudes, talents and values. For example:

➠ Give one or two examples of something you find to be very easy to do at work or in your personal life.

➠ If you had five things to do, all of equal importance, how would you decide what to do first?

➠ If you had three choices of things to do from the list below, which would you do first? Why?

1. Catch up with a co-worker about a project you are working on together.

2. Spend some time thinking through a difficult problem that you need to solve.

3. Finish up a report you've been working on for the last three days.

The first question helps us understand some of the person's talents; things we do with ease are clues to talents. The second question looks at how people establish priorities among equally important tasks, giving clues to what they value. The third question looks at whether the people most like to relate to others, analyze and problem solve or strive to accomplish things. Note that none of the three questions have right or wrong answers.

<u>Strategy #15</u>   Interview and select for skill

In addition to people of quality, you are also looking for people who have the training, knowledge and skill to do the job. Skill or behaviour focused interviews are essential components of any recruitment program.

Using structured interviews where each person is asked a standard set of questions has become common place. If you are not yet using this style of interview, do some reading and learn the value and how-to of this important practice.

Structured interviews should give you two types of information:

➠ specifics of how employees would respond to situations in the future (using hypothetical or situational questions that are job specific)

➠ detailed examples of how employees' behaviour in past situations (using "Tell me about a time when ..." style of questions).

These two types of questions give you important data about behaviours and skills related to the position.

Past behaviour is an excellent predictor of future behaviour. Put another way, if a candidate has never ridden a bicycle then they are not likely to be able to accurately describe exactly how to go about doing this task. If however, they have ridden a bicycle many times, they will be able to describe their skill to you in substantial detail and with ease.

Consider doing situational role-plays during an interview to draw out information about an employee's skills. For example, "Let's suppose I'm your co-worker and you need to give me some critical feedback about how I handled an angry client/customer. Play out what you would say to me." Even though interviews are stressful situations, a skilled candidate will be able to give you a good indication of how she/he would handle the situation in real-life.

Strategy #16   Interview and select for talent

As important as skills are to doing a job well, talents are at least as important. No one would suggest we interview *only* for talent. It is likely equally as limiting to rely exclusively on behavioural or skill-based interviewing. Unlike skills, talents cannot be learned. Talents are our natural leanings. Clues to talents are things we do with ease or excellence without having to practice or without being taught. Doing what we are talented at gives us a sense of satisfaction and strength.

Examples of talents include people who are:

⇒ thinkers, problem solvers or analyzers

⇒ achievers or strivers

⇒ coordinators, arrangers or organizers

⇒ communicators

⇒ connectors (or networkers)

⇒ idea generators or catalysts

⇒ strategizers

⇒ learners.

Effective recruitment requires that a person's talents match the job duties and role she/he will fill in the organization. Miscasting people in jobs that do not match their talent will cause performance management issues down the road.

Here are a few tips for finding talents during interviews:

➤ Listen carefully to the first words in response to a question. The candidate's choice of words and content of the answer may give you clues to their talents. For example, words such as "I feel..." or "The best idea is..." or "One possible solution..." may tell you the person is relationship or connection oriented (I feel), an idea person (the best ideas), or an analyzer and problem solver (one possible solution).

➤ Listen for specific details. Areas of talent often present as specific examples in time, place, person or events. For example, in response to the question, "Tell me about a time you helped solve a difficult problem", a person may relate a story about supporting a co-worker with personal problems. The choice of story and details provided give valuable information about his/her talents (supporter, relater, connector).

➤ Ask unusual questions such as, "Let's suppose you had 15 spare minutes to yourself in an otherwise very busy day. How would you use your time?" The variety of responses will surprise you. Some people may call home, others would read, go for a short walk or catch up with a co-worker. Each response may give you a clue to the person's talents.

➤ Interview current employees who have specific talents you see as desirable. Do some patterns emerge in their answers to common questions? Look for these same types of responses (suggesting the same or similar talents) in your interviews with candidates.

Strategy #17   Partner with other organizations to share recruitment activities

Sharing the work involved with recruitment, screening, interviewing and reference checking not only lightens the load, it also reduces costs and brings fresh perspectives to the process.   One employer may "reject" a candidate while the other may find the candidate matches the skills and talents their organization requires.   The candidate attends only one interview and recruitment time is reduced.   If advertisements or job postings are also shared, both employers save time and money.   Replacing competition with cooperation will no doubt impress prospective employees and may also increase the number of people who apply for available positions.

Strategy #18   Assess how "coachable" an applicant is

Some applicants may not have all the skills necessary for the job.   However, they may have many

> *"There's a little Obi Wan Kenobie in all of us."*
>
> Unknown

talents, good motivation and be quick learners.   These people will likely become exceptional employees if they are "coachable".   Here is a checklist to determine if someone is likely to enjoy the challenges of learning. Is the person:

➔ willing to take risks and make mistakes?

➔ willing to admit errors and explore how to prevent them in the future?

- willing to take advice or critical feedback without becoming defensive?

- likely to take initiative in soliciting help and feedback?

- able to listen to other's experiences and ideas?

- able to build trust-based relationships with co-workers and supervisors?

- prepared to challenge old ways of doing things?

- likely to set high expectations themselves?

- prepared to learn from those who are better trained or more experienced, regardless of age?

- prepared to do regular self-critique?

Strategy #19   Never, never, never …

Here are a few tips that will help you get a good hire every time:

- Never interview alone (always interview with one or two others).

- Never neglect to carefully check references just because the person has a "good reputation" or because you are in a rush.

- Never use letters of reference alone – always make a follow-up telephone call to the writer.

- Never fail to contact former employers (even if the employee has not given a past employer as a reference).

- Never have someone who did not interview the candidate do the reference checks.

➠ Never fill the position with someone you have serious concerns about.

➠ Never let someone else hire an employee who you must supervise without any involvement from you personally at key steps in the process (interviewing and reference checking).

➠ Never hire someone sight unseen because your boss or a co-worker said the person is "just great!"

➠ Never disregard negative references or concerns that arose during the interview; respond to these with additional questions, learning goals or probationary conditions.

➠ Never accept internal transfers of employees who have experienced performance problems in other parts of the organization unless you are *certain* the problems were situational, temporary, or can be managed better in your setting or team.

Finally, never, never, never break any of the above "rules" or you will pay for it in pain and suffering later. If you do break a rule, learn from the experience!

Strategy #20 Apply principle-based analysis of information obtained during interviews and reference checks

Here are a few thoughts to consider when reviewing each candidate after interviews and reference checks are complete.

1. People may or may not change. They can change themselves but we cannot change them. Don't

rationalize hiring someone who you feel needs a major talent or attitude "makeover" before they can be successful in their new role. Be prepared to train for skills but don't expect to change who the person *is*.

2. All behaviour communicates and all behaviour is motivated. Do not assume you know or understand the meaning or motivation of behaviour. If in doubt, ask.

3. Both positive and negative judgements about personal characteristics or appearances will likely prove wrong once you know the person well enough.

> *"In the province of the mind, what one believes to be true, either is true or becomes true."*
>
> John Lily

4. A person's greatest skill is often also one of their primary weaknesses. For example, a person who is organized and efficient may also be rigid, obsessed with order or have expectations that everyone be as organized as she/he is.

5. What a person describes as their most significant successes *and/or* failures gives important clues about their underlying needs or aspirations.

6. Conscious awareness of limitations or weaknesses must precede changes in behaviour. An employee who cannot tell you what they are not good at may lack conscious awareness. The employee will not be able to change or improve what they do not yet understand.

There's more to read:

Ahlrichs, N. (2000). *Competing for Talent: Key Recruitment and Retention Strategies for Becoming an Employer of Choice.* Palo Alto, CA: Davies-Black Publishing.

Arthur, D. (1998). *Recruiting, Interviewing, Selecting and Orienting New Employees.* New York, NY: AMACOM.

Beauregard, M. & Fitzgerald, M. (2000). *Hiring, Managing and Keeping the Best.* Toronto, ON: McGraw-Hill Ryerson Limited.

Buckingham, M. & Clifton, D.O. (2001*). Now, Discover Your Strengths.* New York, NY: The Free Press.

Buckingham, M. & Coffman, C. (1999). *First, Break all the Rules.* New York, NY: Simon & Schuster.

Cook, M. F. (1992). *The AMA Handbook for Employee Recruitment and Retention.* New York, NY: AMACOM.

Deems, R. S. (1999). *Hiring: How to Find and Keep the Best People.* Hawthorn, NJ: Career Press.

Doverspike, D. & Tuel, R.C. (2000). *The Difficult Hire; Seven Recruitment and Selection Principles for Hard-to-Fill Positions.* San Luis Obispo, CA: Impact Publications.

Gubman, E.L. (1998). *The Talent Solution: Aligning Strategy and People to Achieve Extraordinary Results.* New York, NY: McGraw Hill.

Kaplan, D. L. (1996). *The Ultimate Recruitment Guide and Notebook.* Torrance, CA: Griffin Publishing.

Kaye, B. & Jordan-Evans, S. (1999). *Love 'em or Lose 'em: Getting Good People to Stay.* San Francisco, CA: Berrett-Koehler Publishers, Inc.

Wanous, J. P. (1992). *Organizational Entry: Recruitment, Selection, Orientation and Socialization of New Employees.* New York, NY: Addison Wesley Longman.

Getting Off to a Good Start: Orientation and the First Few Months

As is the case with recruitment and selection, many books describe the basic steps of a well-planned orientation program for new employees. Briefly and to refresh the reader's recall, a quality orientation should include:

1. Written Information

    ⟫ organizational history

    ⟫ organizational description (who are your clients/customers, what services/products are provided, locations, number of clients/customers served, number of employees, budget size, governance model and revenue sources)

    ⟫ brochures or other print materials about the organization (e.g. last year's annual report)

    ⟫ organization and department structures

    ⟫ photos of key personnel

    ⟫ a chart describing people (by name), positions and reporting relationships

    ⟫ philosophy, beliefs, values, mission and vision statements

➠ organization's telephone book (including e-mail addresses)

➠ policy and procedures (for the organization as a whole and for the area in which the employee will work)

➠ probationary period information (expectations, appraisal process and time frame)

➠ a short employee handbook describing key personnel policies, benefits, payroll periods, commencement and termination procedures, grievance policies, overtime policies, dress code, etc.

➠ job descriptions for the new employee, their supervisor and co-workers whose jobs differ from the employee's own position

➠ day timer or appointment book.

It is an excellent idea to prepare multiple copies of the above items as a package. This saves time and energy when each new person begins. The orientation materials may be sent to the employee a few days before his/her start date so she/he will have time to read and prepare questions to be asked during the in-person orientation.

2. Orientation Activities

➠ overview of orientation process (what will happen in the days and weeks ahead)

➠ payroll commencement forms, timesheets/timecards

➠ discussion regarding philosophy, mission, vision and values of the organization

- discussion re: structure and reporting relationships
- discussion of job description and duties
- discussion of working hours, scheduling, flexibility, overtime requirements
- discussion of benefits (sick time, health care, holidays)
- tours of various facilities in the organization
- meet co-workers, supervisor and clients/customers
- description of support available from supervisor, co-workers, managers, human resources
- description of available training and/or required training to be completed and timelines
- discussion about how to solve problems and where to go for help with questions or problems
- one or more full day orientation shift with on-site guidance of senior co-worker or supervisor
- information about social gatherings, employee networks or other group activities
- answers to employees' questions.

To a large extent this list is a common sense approach to a *technically* good orientation. However overwhelmed the employee may be, the information provided is a necessary part of starting any new job. You may wish to pace the initial orientation activities over a few days to help the employee digest the information in manageable chunks.

A mistake often made by supervisors and managers is to regard the orientation phase as spanning the first few days or perhaps the first week or two on the job. We are so relieved to have hired a good person, we trust they will somehow figure out the job as they go along. Alternately we may leave it to co-workers to show a new employee the ropes, draw them into the team and answer their questions. However, turnover rates among new employees are higher than for any other single group of employees. Clearly we need some innovative strategies to help newcomers find their place and feel a sense of belonging and contribution in their first months on the job.

Strategy #21 Start creating connections before the commencement date

After the new employee has accepted the position (but before she/he begins work) try some of the following ideas.

➠ Ask the senior manager of the organization or department to telephone the employee and welcome him/her to the organization.

➠ Send a welcome card by e-mail or mail from the new team, co-workers and supervisor.

➠ Mail the orientation package and follow-up with a telephone call.

➠ Invite the new employee to a team meeting, staff meeting, training event or social gathering.

➠ Ask one co-worker to make a welcoming telephone call and/or invite the new employee to lunch or coffee.

➠ Have a T-shirt made up with "I belong to_____ now!" and drop it off at the employee's residence.

➠ Send a short home video from the worksite and new team of co-workers. This could be:

◆ a day in the life at your new job

◆ a team meeting

◆ a series of "mugshots" of co-workers, clients/ customers, supervisors and managers.

Strategy #22 Involve shorter-term employees in briefing new employees about what to expect

Involving long-term employees in orientation of new employees is standard operating procedure by most employers. However, involving shorter term employees (e.g. people who have worked for you between six and twelve months) has a number of potential benefits.

This strategy is useful in the first week or two of employment because it helps the employee understand his/her feelings and experiences are probably "normal". Short-term employees will remember these experiences very well. This strategy helps create a "we're all in it together" feeling or "look at us, we made it and you will too." Building a sense of connection among employees is a key factor influencing long term retention.

Strategy #23   Create an orientation treasure hunt

Create a list of information or objects that can only be obtained from specific people or locations in the organization.   The employee must pay a visit to each person or location to collect all the information or objects. Give employees a month or so to complete their treasure hunts.   Make the exercise fun and even a bit silly. Items to be collected could include:

➡ candid photos of all the people who work in the main office

➡ a business card from each manager or supervisor

➡ the number of stairs you have to climb to get to the "top" (i.e. the senior manager's office)

➡ the home telephone number of any employee(s) you care to name

➡ the names and ages of the children of any employee(s) you care to name

➡ the make, model and year of the cars of any employee(s) you care to name

➡ the budget for the new employee's program, department, or site

➡ the name and job title of the longest serving employee in the organization.

Strategy #24   Create a buddy system for new employees

The concept of a buddy system is simple but powerful. People who feel a sense of belonging and significance are likely to stay with us longer. Making a strong personal connection with at least one other human being (other than a supervisor) can create attachments and support retention. The buddy may be a co-worker or peer who has received "buddy training". Being chosen as a buddy can also be a feather in the cap for longer-term employees.

To set up a buddy program:

➠ Gather a group of employees to design the program.

➠ Clearly define the goals of the program (e.g. to create a sense of belonging, reduce isolation, increase support and improve retention).

➠ Develop the role of the buddy (what they will/can do and what their limits are in terms of time or types of problems handled).

➠ Develop a short job description for buddies.

➠ Decide who can participate (*all* new employees or only those who choose to).

➠ Time define the program (e.g. the first three to six months on the job).

➠ Design a short training program or video for buddies so they understand their role and its limits.

A great idea is for each buddy to send a "Glad you're with us" card or e-mail at key times. The times could include:

➤ one month anniversary

➤ completion of probation

➤ completion of all base training

➤ one year anniversary.

A buddy program also decreases the pressure on immediate supervisors of new employees. The buddy and the supervisor share the responsibility to support, guide and encourage the new employee.

<u>Strategy #25</u>   Ensure regular check-ins with the new employee's supervisor

Within the first two weeks of hiring a new employee, the supervisor must set up once weekly contact (at minimum) with the employee. Ideally this contact is face-to-face for at least a half-hour each time. If distance or time does not allow in-person contact, contact should be made by telephone or e-mail. Key items to be covered during this meeting are:

➤ What problems or concerns are arising that the employee is having difficulty solving or managing?

➤ Are any parts of the job or expectations confusing or frustrating?

➤ Are there any parts of the job that the person does not have the skill to perform with confidence?

→ Are there any communication issues at any level or parts of the organization (co-workers, team, management, administration)?

→ What is the employee's general stress level?

→ Are all job expectations clear and reasonable?

→ Is the employee being supported by co-workers?

→ What does the employee need to feel better about his/her new position?

Strategy #26   Be on high alert for problems; practice early intervention

Some employees who leave during their first few months of employment tell of ongoing unresolved frustrations with people, systems and tasks.   This can lead to conflict, breakdown of communication, lack of teamwork, and performance and "attitude" problems.   In some cases, the supervisor or manager is aware "minor" concerns have arisen. In other situations, the supervisor or manager is not aware there are any issues at all until a volcano erupts within the team or until someone resigns.

Practice the following strategies to help resolve problems while they are small and still manageable. Supervisors must:

→ Spend time with new people so they know what employees are experiencing.

→ Listen to and validate concerns no matter how minor they seem.

➠ Help people learn to solve (rather than just identify) problems.

➠ Analyze problem situations as soon as they appear. Determine if the concern is a:

♦ communication problem

♦ performance issue with other staff or the new employee

♦ skill development or training issue

♦ system issue

♦ workload/volume issue

♦ client/customer issue

♦ role or job clarity issue.

➠ Respond to concerns with real action – avoid using words of reassurance to replace active problem solving.

<u>Strategy #27</u>   Emphasize early skill-focused training

You may have hired someone for his/her skills or you may have hired primarily for talent and attitude. Either way the new employee may not have all of the skills needed to do every part of the new job with competence and confidence.

Identify specific areas in which the employee needs skill development. Respond quickly (in weeks not months) by providing:

➠ on-the-job coaching by other skilled workers or by the supervisor

➤ informal training sessions

➤ reading materials, videos or computer instruction

➤ formal practice sessions with immediate feedback to increase skill and confidence

➤ workshops, seminars or courses.

This strategy relies on quick response by the supervisor to meet the needs of new employees. Generalized training will likely miss the mark in terms of skill development. A delayed response may cause employees to think their supervisors or managers don't understand or don't care enough to make individual training needs a priority.

<u>Strategy #28</u> Make stress management training mandatory for all new employees

The nature of work and life is that we will experience stress. Unmanaged, unresolved, high level stress causes *distress* with a host of unpleasant symptoms. Stress related physical and emotional complaints are leading causes of lost days, injuries on the job, conflict among employees and with clients/customers.

An effective stress management program should include teaching employees:

➤ how to change or influence situations (e.g. systematic problem solving, open communication and conflict resolution training)

➠ how to change how they think about situations (re-framing training and "don't sweat the small stuff" adjustments)

➠ how to modify physical responses to stress (relaxation training, biofeedback, health, fitness and diet improvements)

➠ how to recognize the danger zone when things may be out of control and professional intervention is necessary.

<u>Strategy #29</u> Provide part-time, casual, relief and contract or seasonal workers with a full orientation

Many of my consulting clients ask what can be done to improve retention among this important group of employees. My answer is often to ask how the organization treats part-time, casual, relief and contract employees *now*?   Their answers are very consistent. This group of employees is treated differently than full-time, permanent or professional employees. This different treatment tells part-time employees they are valued differently than other employees who work more hours. This is despite the fact that:

➠ part-time and contract employees cost the employer the same amount to recruit as most other employees

➠ employers have a heavy reliance on this group to cover key periods of client/customer service every work week

➠ employers expect these employees to be as skilled, reliable and trustworthy as all other employees.

The different treatment often begins at orientation. The point is simple: ensure all levels and types of employees receive a full orientation and have access to the same supports, training and relationships as their full-time and permanent colleagues.

Part-time, relief and contract/seasonal employees are a valuable resource and are worth keeping.   We will discuss how you can work to improve retention of this group of people in Chapter 7.

<u>Strategy #30</u> Evaluate and revise your orientation process at least once a year

The steps for evaluating your orientation program should include:

➠ framing a series of "big picture" questions that need to be answered by the evaluation (e.g. Are new employees staying longer? What are our most effective strategies?)

➠ identifying sources of information that need to be accessed (e.g. new employees, co-workers, buddies, supervisors, co-workers, managers and clients/customers)

➠ designing tools to gather information (e.g. surveys, interview format, discussion group questions)

➠ gathering the information

➠ summarizing the feedback and making recommendations for change

➠ implementing the changes necessary and tracking the results in the months and year ahead.

There's more to read:

Arthur, D. (1998). *Recruiting, Interviewing, Selecting and Orienting New Employees.* New York, NY: AMACOM.

Beauregard, M. & Fitzgerald, M. (2000). *Hiring, Managing and Keeping the Best.* Toronto, ON: McGraw-Hill Ryerson Limited.

Deems, R. S. (1999). *Hiring: How to Find and Keep the Best People.* Hawthorn, NJ: Career Press.

Kaye, B. & Jordan-Evans, S. (1999). *Love 'em or Lose 'em: Getting Good People to Stay.* San Francisco, CA: Berrett-Koehler Publishers, Inc.

Wanous, J. P. (1992). *Organizational Entry: Recruitment, Selection, Orientation and Socialization of New Employees.* New York, NY: Addison Wesley Longman.

Supervisors: A Vital Link in the Retention Chain

It should be clear from our discussion thus far that supervisors and managers both play a vital role in creating a quality workplace. If you review the list of factors (Chapter 2) that influence job satisfaction, you will note many are either supervisory responsibilities or can be directly influenced by supervisors.

If you are a new supervisor, it is recommended that you pick up a copy of my earlier book, *The Supervisor's Big Book of Answers (1999)*. Order forms are included at the end of this book. There are also many other excellent books on supervision available at your local bookstore.

This chapter presents fifteen strategies to assist supervisors in improving the quality of the workplace and employee retention.

Research has demonstrated the amount and quality of supervisory contact, supervisor's leadership style, skill and experience all impact on employees' decisions to remain on the job for the long term.

25 Things Supervisors Can Do to Improve Retention

Before we turn to specific strategies, let's look at a list of 25 things supervisors can do to positively influence retention.

1. Hire the right person.

2. Provide a thorough and timely orientation.

3. Create a sense of belonging among all employees.

4. Encourage the development of constructive and supportive relationships among co-workers.

5. Have regular, planned/scheduled (ideally face-to-face) contact with employees.

6. Give regular positive feedback regarding performance and contributions.

7. Recognize and reward success in a variety of ways.

8. Give direct, honest and constructive critical feedback when necessary.

9. Demonstrate effective problem intervention.

10. Resolve conflict using win-win solutions.

11. Create flexibility with tasks and schedules.

12. Make exceptions and bend rules when the situation requires.

13. Recognize individual talents and gifts of each employee; match job roles with talents.

14. Raise the bar. Set high, achievable expectations and communicate them clearly.

15. Support employees to succeed using training, coaching and mentoring.

16. Model open, honest, frequent communication; always listen to understand.

17. Share power.

18. Involve employees in decisions that affect them.

19. Accept feedback.

20. Acknowledge mistakes and learn from them.

21. Manage change skillfully.

22. Provide meaningful, constructive, "no surprise" performance appraisals.

23. Respond quickly and supportively to performance issues.

24. Support employees during personal problems or crises.

25. Help employees achieve career and educational goals.

15 Things Supervisors Do That Will *Increase* Turnover

On the flip side of the coin, here are 15 supervisory behaviours that negatively influence employee job satisfaction and morale and therefore, increase turnover.

1. Misusing positional power or authority (use of autocratic or authoritarian "leadership" styles).

2. Having unclear or unreasonably high expectations.

3. Failing to make decisions or delaying decisions unnecessarily.

4. Long absences and/or having minimal contact with individual employees or with the work group/team.

5. Resisting change or managing change ineffectively.

6. Failing to accept or respond to constructive critical feedback.

7. Voicing negative attitudes toward management or toward the organization as a whole.

8. Treating employees harshly or unfairly.

9. Rigidly and/or unreasonably interpreting or enforcing policies or procedures.

10. Indirect or dishonest communication.

11. Failing to follow through on promises or commitments.

12. Failing to effectively manage employee performance problems.

13. Over-involvement in employees' jobs or taking over previously delegated tasks (micro-managing).

14. Over-using critical feedback and under-using rewards and recognition.

15. Treating some employees preferentially.

It is impossible to read these two lists without thinking: "Wow, this is a really tough job." Indeed, there is a great deal riding on supervisors doing their jobs well. As a result, there is also great potential for supervisors to have direct positive impact on employee retention.

Strategy #31 Ensure all supervisors and managers develop competence and confidence

Many supervisors and managers have come up through the ranks or have built a career path based on technical or professional competence in areas other than supervision. This means they are highly skilled at many things other than being a supervisor. Many long-term supervisors have learned from the "fly by the seat of your pants" school of supervisory development.

The skilled supervisor of the future will be required to master a fairly long list of rather complex skills. Formal training, coaching and ongoing support should be available to them in the following areas:

➡ effective and systematic problem solving (especially in group situations)

➡ small and large group facilitation and meeting management

➡ mentoring

➡ team building

➡ employee discipline

➡ presentation skills

➡ teaching (group and individual adult education techniques)

➠ change leadership and transition management

➠ performance management

➠ situationally appropriate use of leadership styles (e.g. coaching, delegating, directing, participating)

➠ conflict resolution (mediation skills).

Formal classroom style training (e.g. workshops, courses or

> **"The aim of education is not knowledge, but action."**
>
> Unknown

seminars) in these areas is not sufficient. This type of training certainly increases knowledge, however, to create *skill, competence and confidence* most supervisors require practice, mentoring and follow-up support.

<u>Strategy #32</u> Build strong relationships, bonds and trust among employees at all levels

Generation X and NinGen employees will demand their workplaces provide them with opportunities to build strong and sustaining relationships. This does not mean work relationships replace family or other friendships. To the contrary, these two generations of employees strongly value life-work balance. The need for relationships at work means we must create a sense of community based on mutual caring and support.

Relationships and trust are created by:

➠ making promises and keeping them ("walking your talk")

➠ spending time with all the people you supervise

- treating people with respect and fairness in all circumstances

- encouraging truth-telling and meaningful dialogue

- creating safety for open communication.

Strategy #33   Create a mentoring program

Think for a moment about someone in your life who has been your mentor. How important has she/he been to you, your career or family life? What have you learned as a result of your mentor's presence and influence?

A mentor can make a significant difference for employees who are new, who are struggling with some aspect of their duties, or who want to learn and grow in their work lives. Employer sponsored mentoring has been shown to double the number of people who intend to stay with their employer for another year or more (Kaye and Jordan-Evans, 1999).

"Someone who gets no help makes no progress."
Unknown

There are several options for how to approach a mentoring program:

- create an informal network of mentors and employees

- as a supervisor, become a mentor

- invite individual interested employees to find their own mentors (inside or outside the organization)

- create a formal mentoring program.

The latter option is more labour intensive but may also provide significantly more benefits in exchange. The steps for creating a more formal program include:

➤ consulting with employees regarding what their needs are and how some of these needs could be met by mentoring

➤ developing a role description for mentors and for protégés

➤ developing guidelines for how protégés and mentors will be matched

➤ preparing a training program for mentors so they understand their role and its limits

> *"Keep company with those who may make you better."*
>
> English saying

➤ creating a few matches to pilot the new program; invite feedback from the mentors and protégés and make adjustments to the program

➤ advertising the program internally; be clear about what mentors and protégés can reasonably expect of each other (time commitments, roles, limitations, boundaries).

The role of a mentor includes:

➤ providing individual work-related support (problem solving, guidance, stress management, etc.)

➤ providing coaching or teaching on tasks

➤ encouraging and rewarding skill development, risk taking and growth

➤ supporting taking responsibility for and learning from mistakes

➠ holding up a mirror for the protégé to increase self-awareness and personal growth

➠ supporting career development and goals.

Mentors give of their time and wisdom. However, their relationships with protégés are mutually beneficial. For many skilled or senior employees, being asked to advise, support and guide is rewarding and fulfilling. Best yet, being part of a mentoring program strengthens the ties people have with each other. Strong relationships are vital to a healthy workplace.

Strategy #34 Work toward supporting family life and work life as parts of the whole

Many contemporary authors are challenging the notion that employees should not "bring their personal lives to work." If you consider this old axiom, it is quite ridiculous. The idea implies that employees should live compartmentalized existences where home and family never meets work and colleagues. Our personal lives and families have made many compromises in favour of our work lives and careers. It is, therefore, reasonable to expect employers to make certain compromises so we can meet our personal and family needs.

> *"Live for another if you wish to live for yourself."*
> Seneca

For supervisors, this means being flexible in several different ways:

➠ allowing employees to make reasonable changes to schedule or working hours

105

➤ broadening illness leave rules to include illnesses of family members and pets

➤ when circumstances necessitate, allowing children to be present at work for short periods of time

➤ creating team-based support for family or personal emergencies

➤ decreasing required overtime by employees with young families.

A small percentage of employees may take advantage of supervisor and employer flexibility. These situations should be dealt with firmly, directly and on an individual basis. Resist the temptation to reduce flexibility for everyone based on the behaviour of a small number of employees who may abuse their privileges.

<u>Strategy #35</u> Treat every person as special and different

This strategy also challenges traditional management thinking that supervisors must treat everyone the same. Everyone should be treated with fairness and respect. However, making exceptions, bending rules and treating people as unique and special is essential for creating quality workplaces.

Supervisors are sometimes reluctant to use this strategy because they fear employees will take advantage of the new flexibility or individual considerations will be abused. Employees will soon come to understand that *everyone* will receive some recognition, a special break or two, perks and opportunities. Examples include:

➠ time off on the employee's birthday or anniversary

➠ extra training or benefits than what is normally available

➠ opportunity to be in an acting supervisory position during short absences of the supervisor

➠ plum assignments, projects or travel opportunities

➠ extra paid time for completing work that is a priority

➠ attendance at conferences

➠ opportunities to try out other positions (e.g. job rotation or job shadowing)

➠ opportunities to take on new responsibilities

➠ opportunities to serve on committees inside or outside of the organization

➠ opportunities to attend management or board meetings.

This is not a strategy reserved for "preferred" employees. It creates a big circle of people who know they are individually valued, understood and appreciated. The small number of people who may take advantage of this responsive environment need to be given feedback about their behaviour and disciplined if necessary. Experience also suggests their co-workers will likely put significant pressure on these employees to not jeopardize the "program" for the whole team or work group.

Strategy #36 Look for opportunities for employee input into decisions that affect them

The principle underlying this strategy is that employees will support what they help create. If the decision has direct impact on certain individuals or groups, their advice and opinions are essential. Supervisors and managers need to make genuine efforts to consider employees' input when making decisions. Create a climate of safety so employees can be open and honest. **Never** create negative consequences or retaliate when employees make suggestions with which supervisors or managers disagree.

> *"People don't resist their own ideas."*
>
> Unknown

Employee input must be regarded as desirable, valuable and necessary for quality decision-making. This doesn't mean, however, that managers or supervisors relinquish their responsibility to make decisions based on broader considerations or information. If employee concerns or preferences cannot be fully represented in a final decision, the supervisor must explain why.

When gathering input, supervisors must skillfully facilitate any group meetings of employees. Without facilitation, group meetings can become non-productive sessions that focus on problem finding rather than problem solving.

Strategy #37   Set high, clear, achievable expectations

High standards for performance encourage employees to create excellence in their work. High expectations must also be:

➤ clearly communicated so employees understand what the standards are and why they are important

Raise the bar. We never do our very best when others expect little of us.

➤ reasonable for the majority of employees to achieve with good effort and use of their skills

➤ related to organization, team, department or program goals

➤ supported with coaching to encourage success

➤ rewarded and/or recognized generously when accomplished.

The following cautions regarding setting high expectations should be considered by supervisors.

➤ Unrealistically high expectations (those that are unachievable or only achievable by exceptional employees) are likely to lower morale and create resentment.

➤ Expectations that are unreasonable or cannot be easily understood, may be actively resisted by employees.

➠ High expectations set without support, training or coaching needed by employees to succeed, will likely result in unnecessary and costly mistakes.

➠ Excessive use of authority or positional power to impose high expectations will result in conflict, uprisings, dissatisfaction and increased turnover.

"Good is not good where better is expected."

Thomas Fuller

➠ Expectations that are driven by a personal agenda or not focused on meaningful goals will be either ignored or resisted by employees.

Strategy #38 Be creative and generous with positive feedback, recognition and rewards

The majority of employees do their jobs well. Many are exceptional in one or more aspects of their work. However, researchers have found that 95 percent of the feedback employees receive is negative or critical (Lauer and Gebhardt, 1997).

"Good words are worth much and cost little."

George Herbert

It is important to recognize both:

➠ specific accomplishments (goals met, outcomes achieved, projects completed, etc.) *and*

➠ general contributions made by employees (e.g. supporting co-workers, excellence in client/customer service, going the extra mile during a difficult time).

Rewards are tangible things and recognition is symbolic. To be effective all types of rewards or recognition must be:

⇒ appreciated, valued, wanted or needed by the individual employee or by the work group/team

⇒ timely (delays decrease impact)

⇒ sufficient (small trinkets given for big effort send the wrong message)

⇒ genuine and heartfelt

⇒ broadly available across all levels and types of positions

⇒ specific (connected to what the employee has actually done or contributed)

> *"Create a big circle of winners. Heroes can exist in any role."*
>
> Unknown

⇒ frequent enough but not so frequent that they lose value

⇒ varied over time (as the saying goes, no one wants "too much of a good thing").

It is also important to reward and recognize the "right" things. These include:

⇒ solved (rather than identified) problems

⇒ learning and curiosity

⇒ long term and win-win solutions

⇒ increased awareness and growth

⇒ teamwork, partnerships, collaboration and cooperation

⇒ creativity, entrepreneurship and appropriate risk taking

⇒ accepting responsibility and taking leadership

➠ effectiveness and good decision-making under pressure or during crises

➠ issue prevention

➠ early intervention on issues.

Monetary rewards are both wanted by employees and potentially dangerous. For example, year-end bonuses that are given to everyone are likely not rewards (i.e. they are not connected to specific behaviours or contributions). They will likely be seen as entitlements or gifts rather than being signs of appreciation for effort made on behalf of the organization. On the other hand, monetary rewards given only to selected employees may be resented by those who do not receive the reward. This can lead to hard feelings among co-workers and negative feelings toward managers who made the decision.

> *"Everyone who does the best he can is a hero."*
>
> Josh Billings

Consider the following tips for using rewards and recognition effectively.

➠ Involve both individual employees and work groups or teams in describing what they value, want or need as rewards and recognition.

➠ Always use different strokes for different folks (e.g. public acknowledgement will be appreciated by some and will embarrass others).

➠ Be creative in how people are appreciated; small personalized gestures from the heart can say volumes.

→ Say "thank you" frequently and genuinely.

→ Emphasize how people have helped co-workers, clients/customers and supervisors.

→ Ask peers to nominate each other for recognition or awards.

→ Be quick and spontaneous.

→ Be creative.

→ Be generous – what goes around comes around!

→ Ensure senior management plays an active role in any reward or recognition initiatives.

Strategy #39   **Respond to performance problems quickly, supportively and professionally**

Over the past decades, I have lead hundreds of training sessions for thousands of supervisors. When I ask participants to discuss supervisory challenges, many describe performance issues with a specific employee. These problems are often described as long standing and as difficult to approach. The impact of unresolved performance issues includes:

→ decreased quality of client/customer service or productivity

→ decreased morale among the team or work group

→ increased frustration and periodic eruption of full blown conflict

→ increased turnover among frustrated co-workers.

Performance issues require supervisors to use positional power to give feedback and pursue solutions. Solutions to performance issues must be tailored to fit the situation. Performance problems, therefore, require careful analysis. Ask the following questions before giving constructive critical feedback, verbal or written warnings:

> *"It is important to let people know what you stand for. It is equally important that they know what you won't stand for."*
>
> Unknown

- Specifically, what behaviours does the employee have or not have, that is raising concern?

- Do I have all the information necessary?

- Is the information reliable (based on my own or another trustworthy employee's observations)?

- Is the issue related to lack of skill?

- Has the employee demonstrated better or adequate performance or ability in the past?

- Is the employee already aware of the concern? (i.e. has anyone given them feedback?)

- If the employee has received feedback, how did they respond?

- Does the employee appear angry or fearful?

- Could the performance issue be related to health, addictions, abuse or other family or personal issues?

- Does the employee have talent in the area of the performance concern? (Areas of non-talent often appear as performance issues.)

➠ Am I making any assumptions? What information do I need to check these assumptions out?

When responding to performance issues try the following strategies:

➠ Address the issue immediately, face-to-face, and directly (don't sugar coat the feedback).

➠ Be professional; plan what you are going to say and choose a private location.

> *"The successful manager must be a good diagnostician and must value the spirit of inquiry."*
>
> Edgar Schein

➠ Keep the feedback meeting short and behaviour specific; do not comment on attitudes. ("Attitude" is inferred from your observations of employee's behaviour.)

➠ Ask questions and listen carefully to the information provided by the employee.

➠ Ensure the employee understands his/her performance or behaviour must change immediately and for the long term (i.e. cycles of improvement followed by return of the poor performance are not acceptable).

➠ Fit the corrective feedback to the mistake or situation. Use constructive critical verbal feedback for minor situations. Use verbal or written warnings for more serious or repeated performance issues.

➠ Set specific expectations (what the employee must do or not do and by when); ask the employee for a commitment to work toward improved performance.

➠ Identify what training, mentoring, coaching, counselling or other supports the employee needs to be successful.

➠ If required by policy or for legal reasons, document the meeting. Verbal or written warnings must be documented and placed on the employee's personnel file.

➠ Plan to follow up as often as necessary.

➠ Encourage the employee as she/he makes efforts to improve; encourage co-workers to support these improvements as well.

Readers are advised to consult *The Supervisor's Big Book of Answers* for a detailed, step-by-step approach to giving constructive critical feedback and conducting performance related discipline.

Strategy #40   Develop a strong support network among employees

Co-workers and supervisors are often in a better position than friends and family to provide support. Co-workers understand the nature of stressors at work and can be supportive without requiring the employee to explain the nature of the work or its frustrations. The goal of creating a strong support network is to help employees solve work-related problems, decrease job stress and decrease feelings of isolation.

A strong support network:

➤ gives employees opportunities to "vent" followed by constructive problem solving and assistance with resolving conflict

➤ gives empathy and understanding about problems and stressful situations

➤ creates friendships and/or strong collegial relationships at work

➤ allows debriefing of crises, stressful events or difficult situations after they are experienced

"Try to give people as much as they need. Tomorrow you may need it back."

Unknown

➤ encourages open dialogue and honest discussion about events or problems

➤ may be one-on-one or group based.

A support network is *not:*

➤ a vehicle for complaining about situations without any effort to address them constructively

➤ a management supported grapevine

➤ a clique that supports some, but not all, employees.

Create a support network that provides three different types of support:

1. Informational support: training, role clarification, problem solving, ways of managing stress, mentoring, coaching.

2. Emotional support: empathy, caring trust, acceptance, love, reassurance, fun, social contact, story-telling.

3. Task support: sharing the load, giving resources, flexibility with tasks, scheduling duties.

Strategy #41 Involve employees in developing operating guidelines for their work site, team or department

Each team, workgroup or location should have its own set of guidelines for efficient and effective operations. These should be developed:

➭ by the team and the supervisor

➭ in conjunction with other sites or teams doing similar work

➭ in coordination with organizational policies and procedures (to ensure no inconsistencies or contradictions)

➭ using a simple structure and plain language.

Ensure an annual review and update takes place to keep guidelines current.

There is a tendency to set a rule for every possibility. This amounts to trying to legislate common sense. Employees should be encouraged to learn from mistakes by taking ownership and identifying preventive future actions. Employees must have guidelines that give them essential direction and clarity on program, team or site operations.

It is no more rational to create a new rule after every mistake than it is to remove a rule after every success.

However, people should still be encouraged to think, problem solve, be creative, consult each other and use good judgement. Therefore, don't over-regulate or over-control.

Emphasize self-regulation and clear thinking rather than compliance with rules.

Some supervisors set up new procedures after an employee makes a mistake. Shutting the barn door after the horse is out has long been recognized as futile. If a new procedure is needed to prevent future *serious* incidents or problems from occurring, then this is a good idea. Developing rules after *minor* issues or problems occur is likely an over-reaction and will negatively impact all employees' autonomy and job flexibility – these two factors are key in ensuring job satisfaction and high retention.

<u>Strategy #42</u> Enrich jobs, offer challenges and encourage skill development

Job enrichment helps employees use their talents and abilities to go beyond the duties of their regular job. Most employees enjoy learning new skills and stretching their existing skills. Employees who perform their jobs well may need something more to keep them satisfied and interested in staying. Wise supervisors work with employees to create these opportunities.

"The greatest pleasure in life is doing what people say you cannot do."

Walter Bagehot

Supervisors must consult each individual before embarking on a program of challenges or new opportunities. Some employees value stability, consistency, and predictability. As a result, these folks will react with fear or anxiety when presented with challenges too far outside their comfort zone.

There are many ways of enriching a job. Use the following tips as a guide.

➠ Ask employees what aspects of their talents or abilities could be more fully used by the organization.

➠ Increase the level of independence and autonomy within employees' current duties (i.e. the supervisor identifies *what* must be accomplished and employees determine *how* they will achieve the required outcome).

➠ Provide opportunities for employees to act in temporary supervisory or team leader positions.

➠ Offer employees opportunities to rotate to other positions inside the organization - usually to other programs, departments or locations.

➠ Offer employees opportunities to work on committees, projects or with senior managers.

➠ Increase employees' profile by offering work involving leadership responsibilities (e.g. chairing a committee, special event, or project task team).

"You must not expect old heads upon young shoulders."
English proverb

➠ Offer opportunities for being involved from start to finish with a task, rather than being responsible for only part of a task.

➠ Invite employees to become mentors, coaches or buddies involved in orienting and training new employees.

➠ Offer Train the Trainer courses, then involve employees as internal educators with peers.

Strategy #43 Offer training in 3 key areas: stress management, problem solving and conflict resolution

Stress management programs are essential for employees to be able to handle the everyday events of their lives at work and at home. An effective program should include skill development in:

➡ how to change situations and solve problems that are causing stress

➡ how to change their physiological responses to stress

➡ how to change how they think about events in their lives

➡ follow-up coaching or support to ensure knowledge is applied on the job.

Training for effective problem solving should include:

➡ developing analytical skills for problem/issue identification and definition

➡ a systematic approach or model of problem solving

➡ case studies as practice sessions that simulate real life or real work experiences

"The great difficulty in education is to get experience out of ideas".

George Santayana

➡ practicing problem solving in both group and individual situations on the job.

Training for conflict resolution should include:

➠ increasing awareness and insight about how we have learned to deal with conflict

➠ understanding traditional approaches to conflict and why these are not successful in resolving most conflict

➠ information and practice using interest-based negotiation (also called principle-based or mediation) to create win-win solutions

➠ guided practice or coaching to ensure knowledge is applied on the job.

As noted previously, supervisors must first develop skill and confidence in facilitating and supporting employees to manage stress, solve problems and resolve conflict.

<u>Strategy #44</u> Embrace and celebrate diversity

Our workforce is increasingly comprised of a wonderfully diverse group of employees. Diversity may include differences in:

➠ gender (e.g. women or men working in non-traditional occupations)

➠ culture and language

➠ race

➠ religion

➠ sexual orientation

➠ disabilities

➠ disciplines or professional backgrounds

➠ age and generation.

When managed well, workplace diversity brings with it many opportunities. Books on this topic abound and it is recommended the reader further explore the topic before creating formal workplace diversity strategies. However, the following tips will help you get started:

➠ Acknowledge and talk openly at all levels about how diverse your workforce is.

➠ Identify the advantages and benefits of working within a multilingual, multicultural, multiracial environment.

➠ Invite people to share life and personal histories with co-workers at appropriate moments.

➠ Encourage learning among employees of different backgrounds.

➠ Create opportunities for sharing that are safe and fun (e.g. multicultural potluck lunches or learning words and sentences in several languages).

➠ Invite interested employees to present short workshops, or travelogues about their life experiences, traditions or culture.

➠ Create opportunities for meaningful dialogue among employees. Invite them to explore common ground and experiences as well as explore how their differences impact on how they do their jobs, relate to authority, serve clients/customers or respond to problems.

➠ Create assertive policies to help prevent discrimination.

➠ Ensure quick and assertive management responses to incidents or problems related to discrimination.

➠ Practice zero tolerance for employee behaviour that is disrespectful, narrow or intolerant.

<u>Strategy #45</u> Create a healthy, safe, and efficient working environment

Aspects of the physical environment include:

➠ access to materials and supplies needed to do the job

➠ safe equipment and facilities

➠ necessary equipment is readily available and in good repair

➠ facilities that are comfortable (have the necessary furniture, work space, telephones, washrooms, meeting rooms and are adequately heated and cooled)

➠ access to reference materials or other resources

➠ availability of privacy or quiet work space if/when needed.

Attending to "the basics" helps employees to focus on doing their jobs well. When necessary, supervisors must play an advocacy role within organizations to ensure employees have these essential elements. Ask employees to identify aspects of their physical environment that are unsafe or insufficient. Work quickly to improve the situations they identify.

There's more to read:

Bell, C.R. (1998). *Managers as Mentors: Building Partnerships for Learning.* San Francisco, CA: Berrett-Koehler Publishers.

Billings-Harris, L. (1998). *The Diversity Advantage: A Guide to Making Diversity Work.* Oak Hills, CA: Oak Hill Press.

Boyle, D.C. (1997). *Secrets of a Successful Employee Recognition System.* Portland, OR: Productivity Press Inc.

Cunningham, J.B. (1998). *The Stress Management Sourcebook.* Lincolnwood, IL: NTC Publishing Group.

Dana, D. (2000). *Conflict Resolution.* New York, NY: McGraw Hill.

Fisher, S.G. (1997). *Manager's Pocket Guide to Performance Management.* Amherst, MA: Resource Development Press.

Hackman, R. (1999). *Groups That Work (and Those That Don't): Creating Conditions for Effective Teamwork.* San Francisco, CA: Jossey-Bass.

Hirsh, S.K. (1996). *Work it Out: Clues for Solving People Problems at Work.* Palo Alto, CA: Davies-Black Publishing.

Knowdell, R.F. (1996). *Building a Career Development Program: Nine Steps to Effective Implementation.* Palo Alto, CA: Davies-Black Publishing.

MacLennon, N. (1995). *Coaching and Mentoring.* Ottawa, ON: Renouf Publishing Co.

Pfeiffer & Company Staff (1997). *Improving Problem Solving Skills.* San Francisco, CA: Jossey-Bass Inc.

Sonnenschein, W.H. (1997). *Workforce Diversity.* Lincolnwood, IL: NTC Publishing Group.

Stitt, A. (1998). *Alternate Dispute Resolution for Organizations: How to Design a System for Effective Conflict Resolution.* New York, NY: Wiley & Sons Inc.

Whiteman, T. & Verghese, S. & Petersen, R. (1996). *The Complete Stress Management Workbook.* Toronto, ON: Harper Collins Canada Ltd.

Workplace Quality and the Role of Managers

Chapter 7

As we've seen, supervisors and managers play a vital role in improving job satisfaction and increasing employee retention. Senior managers must also work to set the tone, remove barriers and allocate human and financial resources to improve employee retention. In this chapter we will discuss ways for organizational leaders to support creation of a stable workforce of skilled and satisfied employees.

Perhaps the greatest contribution senior managers can make is to set the tone of retention efforts. Keys to setting the tone include:

➠ communicating optimism that employee retention can be improved with concerted and coordinated efforts

➠ supporting creativity in developing retention strategies at all levels and in all areas of the organization

➠ securing necessary human and monetary resources to support retention activities

➠ removing attitudinal and policy barriers that may stumble retention initiatives.

There are several commonly held beliefs about turnover that have almost reached mythic status. The following ten commonly held beliefs, or "turnover myths", must be challenged by managers at all levels in the organization for retention strategies to have the desired positive impact.

Myth 1. Turnover is caused *primarily* by external rather than internal (organizational) factors.

Myth 2. Low compensation is *the primary* cause of turnover.

Myth 3. Most people leave because their work is not valued by society, is too routine, or there is no career ladder.

Myth 4. Most people leave because they find more challenging jobs for higher pay and better benefits.

Myth 5. Nothing can be done about turnover except to learn to live with it.

Myth 6. Retention efforts will cost more than they are worth.

Myth 7. Current labour shortages will be short lived, therefore, retention efforts will prove to be unnecessary.

Myth 8. Losing an employee doesn't really hurt the organization very much.

Myth 9. It is easier to replace people than it is to try to keep them.

Myth 10. Most of the employees who leave are not the organization's "best people".

Strategy # 46 **Include employee retention in annual operational and long range strategic planning**

As we discussed in Chapter 1, retention will not happen by accident – it will happen *by plan.* Among my 60 plus organizational clients, only a handful have created specific operational and long-range strategic goals to improve employee retention. Most organizations that have a plan are just beginning to implement specific targeted strategies to reach their retention goals.

Developing a comprehensive retention program includes the following steps:

➡ analyzing current turnover rates and setting retention targets for each department, program, location, key vulnerable positions and for the organization as a whole

➡ estimating current costs of avoidable turnover

➡ developing written goals spanning three to five years

➡ surveying employee satisfaction to identify specific areas of concern

➡ creating strategies and initiatives to address concerns identified by employees and by the turnover analysis

> *"I must hurry up and catch up with the others, for I am their leader."*
>
> T-shirt wisdom

➡ identifying cost savings when retention targets are reached

➡ allocating both human and financial resources to retention

- ➠ providing training and support to supervisors

- ➠ establishing timelines for initiatives to be implemented and for completion of major goals.

It is also an excellent idea to name the organization's retention program. An internal contest to name the program may result in some very creative suggestions from employees and supervisors!

It is essential to involve supervisors in each step of the process of developing the plan and creating the specific initiatives. Retention activities need to be customized to fit the differing needs and challenges of each department, program or area of the organization. Adopting a "one size fits all" approach will likely decrease the effectiveness of retention efforts.

"Above all, challenge yourself."

Unknown

In addition to being customized, activities should prioritize vulnerable areas identified in the turnover analysis. The research literature suggests employees who have the highest turnover are:

- ➠ part-time, casual and relief personnel

- ➠ new employees

- ➠ younger employees

- ➠ women returning from maternity leave

- ➠ women with pre-school aged children

- ➠ some well educated or highly trained employees.

Finally, it is important to create a leadership team or designate a leadership position for the retention program. If the organization has a personnel or human resource manager, a portion of their time should be designated for planning, supporting and monitoring retention activities. A leadership team should include personnel from all levels in the organization and also representatives from each major department or location.

If this seems like a lot of work – it is! Remember, however, many organizations spend up to ninety percent of their annual operating budgets on human resources. People are our most valuable asset and they are worth our investment of time and money to protect.

Strategy #47   Survey employee satisfaction regularly

High levels of employee satisfaction are correlated with higher employee retention. Regularly surveying employees about their satisfaction with their work, supervisory support, organizational policies and working conditions is an important part of any retention program.

"Who sees organizational leadership more clearly than its employees?"

Unknown

A well-designed survey gathers information on much more than employees' satisfaction with "the job". The surveys, therefore, are best called "workplace satisfaction" or "employee satisfaction" surveys.

The benefits of satisfaction surveys are:

➠ communicating to employees that the employer values their input and cares about what employees think about the workplace

➠ communicating the employer's intent to make improvements based on employees' concerns and input

➠ identifying specific target areas for change

➠ maximizing the use of time and money in areas that are likely to have the greatest impact.

Developing A Satisfaction Survey

The steps in preparing to do a satisfaction survey include:

➠ announcing management's plan to survey employees' opinions (what is being done, why, what will be done with results, how employees will be given the results and when)

➠ developing a project leadership team including employee representatives from each organizational level, department or location

➠ reviewing examples of surveys used by other organizations or by your organization in past years

➠ developing a master list of possible questions to ask on the survey

➠ deciding what questions are most important to gather information about (see guidelines in the following section)

- drafting the survey for review by the leadership team and management; ensure the survey uses plain language and questions are clear
- revising the survey based on feedback
- piloting the survey with a small number of employees to ensure instructions and questions are understood
- distributing the survey to all employees; colour code or mark the surveys for specific programs, departments or locations to aid in later analysis
- counting the number of surveys distributed to each area so return rates can be calculated later
- spreadsheeting numerical data and typing written comments
- summarizing numerical data using simple charts/graphs and summarizing themes from written comments
- preparing a final written report with recommendations for activities by management to respond to employees' concerns
- preparing a short summary report for distribution to all employees; make the full report available to anyone who is interested.

Guidelines for Deciding What Questions Are Important

Deciding what questions to ask is crucial to the survey design process. Questions can be grouped into 5 categories.

1. Questions about the demographic profile of employees responding to the survey (age, gender, length of service, program/department assignment, type of position, full/part-time).

2. Job/work specific questions (workload, type of duties, clarity of expectations, variety of tasks, value of work by self/others, challenges).

3. Team or work group specific questions (team work, sharing the load, flexibility, communication, problem solving, conflict resolution).

4. Supervisory questions (quality and quantity of supervision, performance appraisals, feedback, recognition, fairness, personal support, coaching, training, involvement in decision-making, sense of belonging).

5. Organizational questions (compensation, benefits, job descriptions, general policies, personnel policies, hiring and orientation practices, facilities, equipment, technology, materials/supplies, management practices, disciplinary action, recognition and rewards, openness of communication).

Consider the following points when choosing what questions to ask:

⇒ Choose questions that will give valuable and needed information. Choosing questions that would be "nice to know" the answer to will make the survey unnecessarily long.

⇒ Choose questions that management will be able to respond to when the results are known. If you don't want to know the answer to a question, or if there is no intention to do something with the answer, why ask it?

⇒ Choose questions that will be durable over time. Design a survey that can be used for several years, allowing comparison of data from year to year and measurement of improvements in areas of concern.

⇒ Ensure each question asks for information on *one* topic only.

⇒ Ensure the total survey can be completed by employees in 20 to 30 minutes.

Be careful *not to ask* questions that allow individual employees to be identified. The survey respondents should remain anonymous. Asking too many demographic questions may cause employees to believe they can be identified from their responses.

Appendix 2 provides a list of possible questions, sample survey instructions, an idea for an effective format and response scales. Readers are welcome to use this sample survey as a *template* for their own surveys. It is essential that you make changes to the list to fit with your particular situation.

Additional Considerations

1. Remember to leave space for comments at the end of each page or after specific questions likely to generate written responses.

2. Reassure employees their responses will be both anonymous and confidential. Provide envelopes so employees can return their completed surveys.

3. If possible have the surveys received and summarized by someone outside the organization who has no interest in attributing comments or responses to individual employees.

4. Increase return rates by:

    ⤳ creating incentives (one organization gives a lottery ticket to each person who returns their survey by the due date)

    ⤳ giving out surveys at a general staff meeting and asking they be completed immediately

    ⤳ using reminders from supervisors and managers, in person, via memo, e-mail or voice mail

    ⤳ rewarding work groups/teams for having 80 percent return rates or better.

5. Identify employees who may require assistance to complete their survey. This may include:

- employees with low literacy levels

- employees for whom English is a second language

- employees with certain types of disabilities.

6. Establish a contact person to whom employees can address questions or concerns. Track these concerns, inform the leadership team and reflect any significant issues in the final report.

7. Ensure the final report identifies any changes to the survey or survey process for future years.

If You Ask ... You Must Act!

The issues arising from survey results must be reviewed and acted upon by organizational management. Inaction or delayed action will result in employees seeing the survey process as an insincere exercise. Management activities should include:

- full and open discussion of what the information means for the organization in terms of issues and possible changes

- setting priorities among the areas requiring attention

- developing action plans (i.e. *who* will do *what* by *when* and with *what resources?*)

- tracking the implementation of strategies

- surveying employees again one to two years later.

Strategy #48   Focus on why employees are staying (not leaving)

In Chapter 2 we reviewed key factors identified in the literature as reasons employees leave employers. Rarely, however, do we ask our *current* employees what factors influence their decisions to *remain* on the job. Nor do we ask how well we are doing in creating a quality workplace that encourages employees to stay.   Instead, many employers complete interviews or surveys with *exiting* employees. As noted in Chapter 1, the value of exit interviews is somewhat dubious.

There is exceptional value in asking current employees what is important to them in their current jobs, at work sites, with their team and in supervisory relationships.   Like satisfaction surveys, this information will point the way for managers to create initiatives to improve the quality of the workplace *in areas most important to employees.*

This latter point is key. Some research has shown managers tend to emphasize external factors (e.g. competitors, small pools of qualified labour, low wages, absent or poor benefits) beyond their control as reasons for turnover and recruitment problems. In contrast, employees emphasize internal factors (e.g. supervisory support, flexibility, communication, and involvement in decision-making) as primary influences for remaining in a job. These same factors may influence others' decisions to apply for jobs with an organization.

Appendix 3 provides a list of questions and a sample format for a survey about why current employees are staying with your organization. Readers may use this as a template for a similar survey in their organization. You may also want to consider:

- ⇒ interviews or discussion groups with employees about why they stay

- ⇒ asking managers and supervisors to complete the same survey, responding as they think the employees will answer the questions. This will give valuable information about whether managers and supervisors are in touch with what employees value.

Summarize the information received from the surveys and analyze the data in terms of the 10 or 15 factors employees say are most important. Note this survey does not give you information on *how well* the organization is doing in each of these areas. It merely tells you what employees think are the most important factors. You may also want to ask employees to rate (e.g. using a 1 to 5 scale) how well the organization is doing at meeting employees' needs in each of the priority areas identified.

Strategy #49   Review policies and practices - remove barriers and improve flexibility

Policies are essential parts of organizational structure. They give direction, permission and clarity to what must, can or cannot be done by employees. It is wise to regularly review policies and the practices that result from policies. Policy reviews should ask and answer the following questions about key policy areas:

➠ Is the policy necessary?

> *Every organizational policy solves some problems and creates others.*

➠ Is the policy clear? (Will an average employee understand it?)

➠ Is the policy reasonable? (Is the policy overly restrictive or rigid?)

➠ Is the policy current?

➠ Does the policy and current practice match? If not, which should be changed?

➠ Does the policy apply to all or most employees? Was the policy written for a small number of people who make mistakes or take advantage? Was the policy written for the majority of employees who are conscientious and skilled?

➠ Was the policy written following an incident in order to prevent future incidents or restrict employees from certain acts? If so, is the policy still needed and reasonable?

> *Policies must be developed for 95 percent, not 5 percent, of employees.*

➠ Does the policy unnecessarily restrict, limit or create barriers for employee effectiveness?

➠ Does the policy imply employees are not trusted?

➠ Does the policy require multiple levels of approval, decisions, or problem solving?

➠ Does the policy require excessive amounts of paperwork for compliance with things that are relatively minor?

➠ Are all of the policies actually *policies* (i.e. they can only be changed by senior managers or the board of directors) or are they procedures, guidelines or practices that can be changed by supervisors or teams?

➠ Are any policies missing? (Do employees need guidance or clarity in any areas not covered by current policies?)

The process of policy review should include the following steps:

➠ creating an action plan for the process

➠ developing a review team or committee comprised of representatives from each organizational level and department/program or location

➠ consultation with employees about what they see as barriers or unreasonable limits in the current policies

➠ developing policy changes, additions or deletions to improve clarity, increase flexibility, decrease excessive control or rigidity

For some managers "flexible policy" is an oxymoron.

➠ submitting revised policies and/or procedures to senior managers or the board of directors for review and approval.

Addressing Specific Policy Concerns

Attention should be paid to five specific policy areas that are frequently of concern to employees and supervisors.

1. Employee grievance policies should make resources available to employees for conflict resolution at the first stage in the grievance process. Senior employees who have training in interest-based or mediation approaches to conflict resolution should be made available to facilitate meetings between employees or with clients/customers when an issue arises. Alternatively, external mediators or facilitators could be accessed on a fee for service basis to ensure issues are resolved in the earliest possible stage.

2. Benefit eligibility policies should include as many people as possible. Restricting part-time, casual or relief employees from benefits is often done strictly for financial reasons. This is likely a false economy given that employers rely heavily on this group of employees for client/customer service. Each part-time or casual employee costs as much as most full-time or permanent employees to recruit, interview, orient and train. Paying the employer's share of benefits for part-time or casual employees is probably less expensive than having to recruit and train a replacement.

3. Illness leave has traditionally been available only when the employees themselves are unable to work. Many progressive organizations are increasing the flexibility of

sick leave policy to include paid compassionate leave for employees:

➠ to care for family members (children, partners, parents or siblings)

➠ to care for family pets who are ill, aged, etc.

➠ to attend to family crises.

4. Extended health benefits (e.g. dental, vision care, short and long term disability, pension plans, etc.) are usually offered to employees on an all-or-none basis. Despite the substantial costs to employers, not all employees value all components of benefit programs. Depending on their age and stage of life, employees may want or need specific benefits. This suggests employers should offer a flexible menu of benefits that may be chosen by individual employees based on their unique life situation. To illustrate:

➠ Parents of young children may value employer supported childcare over pension, dental or disability benefits.

➠ Employees within 5 - 10 years of retirement may value extra employer pension contributions more than other benefits.

➠ Employees who are assertively pursuing career or educational goals may value additional training or educational sponsorships more than other more conventional benefits.

➠ Employees with ongoing medical concerns may value enhanced health care benefits more than pension, vision or dental coverage.

Creating a menu of desirable benefits should be done in consultation with employees, supervisors and private benefit carriers. It is reasonable to set limits on how much of the organization's resources will be spent on benefits of any type. However, improving the range and flexibility of benefits available could have sustaining positive impact on employee retention.

5. Some organizations have also enhanced employee benefits with creative programs such as:

➠ discount programs with local businesses (e.g. gasoline, car repairs, pharmacies, travel agencies, etc.)

➠ a cookie jar loan program funded by the employer to provide loans of up to $300 once a year to any employee for any reason - no questions asked. Access to the cookie jar is through the employee's immediate supervisor. The employee has up to a year to pay back the loan, no interest is charged and installments are accepted with thanks! Employees must pay back their loan in full before they may borrow from the cookie jar again.

➠ a compassionate fund which is supported by small voluntary donations from employees, friends, family or public donors. Employees are encouraged to donate by payroll deduction. They receive an annual charitable receipt for their contributions. Replacing the normal staff social fund, this program gives $500 (or less) for any reason to any employee on a one time only basis. The money does not have to be repaid.

➠ additional vacation time and opportunities to attend training, conferences or to travel

➠ accrual of extended educational or sabbatical leave time (e.g. 3-6 months) that is "banked" by the employee for each month or year of service.

Strategy #50   Create specific strategies for part-time, relief, casual, and isolated employees

Many employers have a heavy reliance on part-time, casual and relief employees. These people are often called to work on short notice and at odd hours. Many organizations discover turnover rates are higher for part-time, casual and relief staff, as well as for employees who work alone or in isolated locations. Supervisors and co-workers also express concern that these employees do not have a strong sense of belonging with the team or work group.

This essential group of employees must be valued as much as full-time employees working regular hours. This may be a challenge for some employers because long-standing and systematic devaluing of part-time and casual positions has been the norm.

Review the following ideas and strategies as you work to improve retention of this group of employees.

1. Interview or hold discussion groups with part-time, casual, relief and isolated employees. Ask them what they need to improve the quality of their work life.

2. Provide all new employees with a full orientation regardless of their status or number of hours worked.

3. Consolidate several part-time or casual positions into one or more salaried or full-time positions with flexible scheduling expectations.

4. Hold team meetings and training sessions at hours of the day when part-time and casual employees are likely to be available.

5. Ensure supervisors have occasional face-to-face contact as well as telephone and e-mail contact with isolated employees, employees who travel or those who work alone.

6. Ensure all employees receive internal communications (meeting notices, invitations to social events, job postings and training schedules).

7. Create a buddy system matching a full-time employee with a part-time, casual or relief employee. The "full-time buddy" makes regular contact by telephone or e-mail, keeping the part-time employee up-to-date and increasing his/her sense of belonging.

8. Remove barriers in policy, procedures and practice that devalue these employees (e.g. policies or practices that

do not pay part-time or casual staff for attending meetings or training events but do pay their full-time colleagues).

9. Extend partial or full benefit eligibility to part-time and casual employees who have completed a certain length of service.

10. Ensure employees receive recognition and acknowledgement for their contributions in organizational newsletters, at social events and directly from co-workers and supervisors.

11. Actively recruit for full-time positions from employees currently holding part-time and casual positions.

Strategy #51   Create improvements for women with preschool aged children

As noted in Chapter 2, mothers of preschoolers are likely to:

➤ resign their positions in the year after the birth of their babies

➤ change jobs more often

➤ have lower wages.

There is a strong tendency for many employers to regard employees' decisions to leave their jobs to be home with children as examples of *unavoidable* turnover. Some managers regard continuous employment and child-raising as incompatible. It is certainly necessary to respect women's decisions to work at home raising children. However, employers and managers can do a great deal to support women in achieving their career and family goals.

Strategies and policies that support retention of women with young children include:

⮞ reducing required overtime hours

⮞ ensuring reasonable workloads

⮞ providing supervisory support

⮞ providing co-worker support

⮞ working regular evening hours or shifts

⮞ increasing flexibility of working hours or allowing schedule changes

⮞ increasing length of maternity leave available

⮞ working with other women who also have younger children

⮞ support (financial or practical) with finding affordable and safe childcare

⮞ offering a safe, healthy working environment

⮞ providing workshops regarding anticipated adjustments and how to create a support network to employees who are first time parents

⮞ having flexible policies regarding short-term presence of children at work (e.g. during crises or to allow for transportation home by other family members)

➠ if the position allows, telecommuting or different work assignments (e.g. special projects, part-time or flex-time hours).

If a competent and desirable employee resigns her position, it is important to provide a "standing offer" of re-employment when the woman is ready to return to work.

<u>Strategy #52</u> Create an organization-wide training plan

Some employers regard training as a crucial part of providing service to clients/customers. Employees expect both basic training of essential or entry-level skills and advanced training.

A colleague of mine recently told me an interesting anecdote. Faced with a substantial cost estimate from a consultant for several days of proposed employee training, a manager expressed the fear, "What if we do all this training and the employees quit to work somewhere else?" The consultant replied, "Worse yet, what if you don't do the training and they all stay?!"

Whether done internally or by external trainers, training represents a substantial cost for employers. Because of this cost, investing in retaining employees must include a coordinated approach to employee training and development. Many employers have a strictly opportunistic approach to employee training. Some organizations also use employee-specific plans to address performance issues or to improve skills.

An organization-wide training plan requires a more deliberate approach to training. The plan helps ensure limited resources are used to meet both employer and employee priorities for skill development.

Steps for developing a training plan include:

1. Establish employer priorities for required or basic training for all new employees and for employees transferring into different positions. The focus should be on the development of concrete skills required by employees to be successful.

2. Survey employees and supervisors regarding what skills they believe are essential for excellence in job performance.

3. Review employee performance appraisals for all employees to gather information about common training needs.

4. Based on the information contained in Steps 1 through 3, summarize and prioritize training needs for the organization as a whole and for each department, program or location.

5. Assess the best methods of meeting each type of need. Options include: mentoring, individual or group coaching, one-on-one instruction, group-based instruction, classroom style workshops or seminars, practice-style workshops or seminars, formal courses at colleges or universities.

6. Create an annual written training plan matching the training need, employee group/individual, type of training and human and financial resources required.

7. Create an action plan (*who,* will do *what,* by *when,* and with what *resources*) to ensure the goals of the training plan are met.

8. Maximize the use of internal resources to deliver training. This may require some employees build their skill and confidence by attending Train the Trainer courses and by being mentored by skilled, experienced adult educators.

9. Monitor the outcomes of the plan and make adjustments as new needs arise.

10. Annually evaluate each component of the training plan, including employees' and supervisors' perceptions of the quality of various programs, type of delivery used and actual observable improvements in skill or performance on the job.

Employers may also offer other incentives to employees to pursue their own career or professional development goals. These include:

- loans for university or college tuition, books, travel. Loans may be forgiven by the employer upon graduation or based on high academic achievement.

- time-off, with or without pay, to attend courses

- earned educational leave based on length of service or other factors, with/without pay

➠ banking hours annually to be paid as educational leave after several years

➠ external certification programs. Programs or courses are offered by the employer at the work site and are eligible for credits toward post-secondary diplomas or degrees at colleges or universities.

➠ internal certification programs offered by the employer, with incentives or rewards for completion of various levels of training

➠ formal mentoring offered on work time by senior employees to new or less seasoned employees (see Chapter 6 for more detail on mentoring programs).

Remember, training is intended to increase both knowledge and skill. Courses and workshops that increase only knowledge must be followed up with practice sessions, coaching or mentoring to ensure actual skills are solidified through on-the-job experience.

Finally, not all employees will respond to training with changes in their performance, skill or behaviour. Training *will not* likely be successful if employees:

➠ are required to attend training that is not relevant to their actual job duties

➠ are required to attend classroom-style training that does not include job-specific practice components

➠ do not have the talent or interest in developing their skills, even though they may have the ability or potential

➤ have performance problems that are not skill related (e.g. are related to personal problems, addictions, disability, or are "attitudinal").

Strategy #53   Manage change effectively

Given that change in organizations has become so prevalent, it is surprising how little many managers and supervisors know about how to manage change effectively. There are many excellent books, workshops, college and university courses on the topic of change. All personnel in leadership positions would be well advised to become *students of change management* before they become agents or leaders of change. The investment of time will be rewarded with many opportunities to "get it right". As a result, employees will experience positive and well-organized change initiatives, leading to increased confidence in the organization's direction and in its leadership.

Consider the following tips when planning and implementing change inside your organization:

1.   Employees must understand *why* things are changing. Managers must be able to explain, in clear and specific terms:

   ➤ what internal or external factors made the changes necessary (e.g. opportunities or threats)

   ➤ how employees and customers will benefit or be affected

➠ how employees will be involved in the change process.

2.   All change involves ending some ways of doing things and beginning others. Employees may experience loss and grief even if, in the end, they will benefit. Managers must support the grieving process.

3.   Employee involvement should be maximized from the beginning when the change is being conceived – not just during implementation.

> **_Employees will support what they help create._**

4.   Our personal history as children and young adults shapes how we respond to change later in life. No two employees will respond identically as they make their adjustments to change. Support strategies must be flexible to respond to the range of employee reactions during the transition process.

5.   Old cracks in relationships between people, programs or departments will reappear during change. Managers must be prepared to intervene when necessary to resolve these "side issues" so they do not jeopardize the process.

6.   All change processes have periods of chaos or at least of confusion. Employees must be supported as they struggle to make sense of things during difficult times. They need to understand their feelings of uncertainty are normal and transitory.

7. Employee response to change may surface as fear, anger or anxiety about being out of control or even as a sense of pending doom! Managers must listen, validate and support employees to work through these feelings.

    Never:

    ⟫ minimize employee concerns

    ⟫ understate or misrepresent what is actually changing

    ⟫ fail to respond in the hope the concerns will go away.

8. When planned changes are far reaching, there is a tendency for managers to take an incremental approach to the process. They believe that by creating a series of smaller changes, employees will have an easier time making the transition to new ways of work. Unfortunately, the impact is usually the reverse. Employees feel changes seem to be never-ending, disorganized or that managers are not fully disclosing what is being planned.

9. Most change takes more time to complete than originally anticipated. The change event(s) themselves may be relatively short. However, people's adaptation may take considerably longer than expected. Managers must carefully balance patience with persistence. In the absence of a driving force, there is a natural tendency for employees to return to their comfort zone and do things the way they used to do them.

10. During the period of transition following change, some employees may feel "everything is changing". It is very

important for managers to clarify what is changing completely, what will change to some extent and what will change little or not at all. This helps employees have an accurate understanding of what is changing and what is not.

Strategy #54   Invest in career development

In some organizations, career development has come to be synonymous with opportunity for promotion. In fact, career development opportunities can enrich and enhance an employee's range of skills, diversity of experiences and job satisfaction *with or without* promotion. Employers who actively support career development are more likely to have higher employee retention.

Traditional approaches hold that every employee who demonstrates excellence should be considered for promotion. However, as Buckingham and Coffman point out, employees should be able to learn, grow and be challenged without *being required* to move up the career ladder. Employees who demonstrate talent and excellence in *any position* should be valued and challenged as much as employees who have promotion potential.

> *"As long as you're going to be thinking anyway, think big."*
>
> Donald Trump

Although it is beginning to change, in the past, the educational system has been an excellent example of the traditional approach. Some of the best classroom teachers are promoted to vice-principal, principal or administrative positions. Good teachers may or may not have the talent to be good school administrators. Conversely, less skilled teachers who are rarely promoted into leadership positions, may have the talent to become excellent administrators.

Managers of contemporary organizations must create opportunities for employees to develop their skills and remain challenged on the job. For *some* employees this may include mentoring and formal training to prepare them for supervisory, administrative or managerial positions. Helping employees discover their own unique paths is the real work of career development.

Steps for Career Development

1. Establish a career development program that includes guiding principles, key activities and allocates time by supervisors, managers and human resource personnel.

2. Train all those who will be involved in supporting career development with employees.

3. Identify employees who are interested in participating in the program.

4. Establish a schedule for meeting with employees one-on-one at least once per year and as often as once per quarter, depending on the goals and interests of each employee.

5. Ask participating employees to brainstorm lists of things they like and dislike at work, want, or have as goals for their career.

6.   With the employee, identify what his/her talents and skills are.

7.   Ask questions to help discover what the employee's likes, dislikes, wants, talents and skills suggest for future career goals.

8.   Discuss what new experiences, challenges, learning opportunities, training or mentoring would support the employee in attaining his/her goals.

9.   Develop an action plan to support the employee in meeting his/her career goals. Activities could include involvement in projects, job rotation, exchange of personnel with other organizations, acting supervisory positions, course work, job shadowing or increased leadership responsibilities.

A Caveat to Human Services Employers and Employees

A word or two is in order to those readers who work in human services (health care, education, mental health, women's issues, rehabilitation, childcare, etc.). Some managers and supervisors have told generations of employees there is really not a "career" in human services. Most of the managers and supervisors who say this are living proof their statement is untrue. The majority of these managers and supervisors have had rewarding careers spanning several decades. Most have held a diverse series of positions with several different

"Be careful what you wish for ... you might just get it."

Unknown

employers. They have learned, grown and contributed much to the people they serve and to their communities. How else would one define a "career"?

A second commonly held belief is that the people served by human service organizations are often devalued by society. Because their clients live in poverty, have addictions, illnesses, or disabilities, the efforts of employees are also not valued. The work of human service professionals and para-professionals is most certainly valued by clients, their families and by many people in the community at large. It *must* also be highly valued by employers, supervisors and managers. As a result, employees will have reason to be proud of the differences they make in the lives of people who need support. This clearly defines a "career" – and an honourable one at that! Managers and supervisors should use every possible opportunity to reinforce this message. In doing so, they will help employees stay in jobs and in a field that needs many more talented people in years to come.

> *Our work is not always valued by everyone but it is always valued by someone.*

Strategy #55   Make a habit of asking for feedback – learn to listen

As we noted in Chapter 2, managers and employees do not always agree on what is important for creating a quality workplace. As a result, managers must balance their own interests and perceptions with information gathered directly from employees. "Directly" means managers should initiate face-to-face dialogue with employees about topics of concern on a regular basis. Activities could include:

➠ one-to-one interviews with employees at all levels

➠ town hall style meetings between groups of employees and mangers

➠ occasional planned attendance by managers at team, department or site meetings of employees.

The intent of dialogue sessions is for managers to ask questions and employees to answer them. So often, these types of meetings are held so managers can present information or "just wave the flag".

Learning to listen to employees is a key retention strategy for the new millennium. If employees are to be honest, they must feel (and be) safe when discussing concerns and ideas. Employees do not expect every idea to be immediately implemented. They do expect to:

➠ have their ideas listened to and understood

➠ be respected for their efforts to make things better

➠ have their ideas treated seriously

➠ receive feedback about how suggestions were considered when managers made plans or decisions.

Managers must be careful to ask for feedback or input when it is truly wanted and needed. If employees are asked for feedback on a decision that has already been finalized and cannot be changed, then this is not a sincere exercise.

Employees will resent the waste of their time and will distrust future similar requests. They will also come to believe management is patronizing them. Neither of these responses is likely to improve retention.

There's more to read:

Grobman, G.M. (1999). *Improving Quality and Performance in Your Non-Profit Organization: An Introduction to Change Management Strategies for the 21st Century.* Harrisburg, PA: White Hat Communications.

Rothwell, W.J. (1999). *The Action Learning Guidebook: A Real-Time Strategy for Problem Solving, Training Design and Employee Development.* San Francisco, CA: Jossey-Bass.

Rothwell, W.J. (1996). *Beyond Training and Development: State of the Art Strategies for Enhancing Human Performance.* San Francisco, CA: Jossey-Bass.

Spector, P.E. (1997). *Job Satisfaction, Application, Assessment, Causes and Consequences.* Beverly Hills, CA: Sage Publications Inc.

Sturman, G.M. (1993). *Career Discovery Project.* New York, NY: Doubleday

Tieger, P.D. & Barron-Tieger, B. (1995). *Do What You Are.* Boston, MA: Little, Brown & Co.

Concluding Comments

We have now completed our exploration of strategies to improve employee retention. Ahead lies the challenging work of creating an organization-wide retention plan and activities that will bring the plan to reality.

To aid in this process, remember the following key concepts:

➠ Organizational leaders must *believe* they can improve retention and must communicate this belief to everyone involved.

➠ We must define, measure and analyze turnover (or retention) before we try to implement strategies to improve it.

➠ Compensation is only one factor influencing retention – there are many others that we can change or improve.

➠ Current employees are an enormous resource for us in determining what improvements need to be made and what strategies are likely to be most effective.

➠ Employees must be involved in the creation and implementation of any retention program.

➠ Retention strategies must be customized to fit the areas where turnover is greatest; one size will not fit all!

➠ Supervisors are a vital link in improving retention; they must have the skill, time and support necessary to play their roles effectively.

➠ Senior leaders must set the tone and work actively to remove internal barriers for retention activities to be successful.

Finally, let me remind you of a few simple but true observations:

1. We cannot do the same thing over and over and over again and expect a different result.

2. We will always go where we are looking – our beliefs will be manifest in future realities.

3. If nothing changes…nothing changes.

4. Complex problems demand multiple solutions. There is no such thing as a magic bullet that will fix everything at once.

5. Relationships are key to success in life and at work.

Appendix 1

Examples of websites offering job postings for employers and employees:

www.campusworklink.com

www.careeredge.org

www.canada.careermosiac.com

www.charityvillage.com

www.e-cruiter.com

www.hrdc-drhc.gc.ca

www.jobshark.com

www.monster.com

www.netjobs.com

www.workopolis.ca

Appendix 2

Sample Satisfaction Survey

This survey gives you an opportunity to give your opinions about working at (organization). It will take you about 20 minutes to complete. Your responses are anonymous and confidential. The survey will be returned to an external consultant. No attempt will be made to identify you as an individual. If you do not want to answer or cannot answer any of the questions please leave that question blank.

The deadline for surveys to be returned is (date). Please use the stamped return envelope provided.

Survey results will be summarized and this information will be made available to all staff. Your feedback will be used to strengthen and improve the agency and its services.

1. Where do you work in the organization? (check all that apply)

    a. ❑ Administration
    b. ❑ Department A
    c. ❑ Department B
    d. ❑ Department C

2. How long have you worked for (organization)?

    a. ❑ Less than 6 months
    b. ❑ 6 months – 1 year
    c. ❑ 1 to 3 years
    d. ❑ 3 to 5 years
    e. ❑ 5+ years

3. How long do you plan to continue working at (organization)?

    a. ❑ Less than 6 months
    b. ❑ 6 months – 1 yr
    c. ❑ 1-3 years
    d. ❑ 3-5 yrs
    e. ❑ 5+ yrs

4. What is your age range?

    a.   ❑ Under 25 years
    b.   ❑ 26 – 35 yrs
    c.   ❑ 36 – 45 yrs
    d.   ❑ 46 – 55 yrs
    e.   ❑ 56 – 65 yrs
    f.   ❑ 65+ yrs

5. What is your gender?

    ❑ Female   ❑ Male

6. What is your approximate annual income (before taxes and other deductions) from this job, including sleepovers and bonuses?

    a.   ❑ Less than $15,000 per year
    b.   ❑ $15,000 - $20,000 per year
    c.   ❑ $20,000 - $25,000 per year
    d.   ❑ $25,000 - $30,000 per year
    e.   ❑ $30,000 or more per year

7. Is your current position: (check only one)

    ❑   A part-time position   ❑   A salaried position
    ❑   A full-time position   ❑   A casual or relief position

8. In addition to your position(s) at (organization), do you currently work at any other job(s) for other employers?

    ❑   Yes   ❑   No

Please indicate your agreement or disagreement with each statement below.

		Disagree Strongly			Agree Strongly	
9.	I am given enough authority to make decisions in my job	1	2	3	4	5
10.	I feel my job is secure	1	2	3	4	5
11.	My physical working conditions are good	1	2	3	4	5

Any comments relating to this page?

		Disagree Strongly			Agree Strongly	
12.	The amount of work I am expected to do is realistic	1	2	3	4	5
13.	The timelines given to do my work are reasonable	1	2	3	4	5
14.	There are opportunities for promotion if I do good work.	1	2	3	4	5
15.	I can achieve my long term career goals at (organization)	1	2	3	4	5
16.	I feel I am contributing to (organization)'s mission	1	2	3	4	5
17.	I feel part of a team	1	2	3	4	5
18.	I like the people I work with	1	2	3	4	5
19.	My team has common goals	1	2	3	4	5
20.	I am clear on who is my supervisor	1	2	3	4	5
21.	My supervisor's expectations are clear to me	1	2	3	4	5
22.	My supervisor treats me fairly	1	2	3	4	5
23.	My supervisor treats me with respect	1	2	3	4	5
24.	I see my supervisor often enough	1	2	3	4	5
25.	I have the materials and supplies needed to do my job properly	1	2	3	4	5
26.	I have the equipment and access to technology needed to do my job properly	1	2	3	4	5
27.	My supervisor handles any work-related problems with employees well	1	2	3	4	5

Any comments relating to this page?

169

		Disagree Strongly				Agree Strongly
28.	My supervisor handles personal issues with employees	1	2	3	4	5
29.	If my work needs improvement, my supervisor tells me directly and in a professional manner	1	2	3	4	5
30.	My supervisor gives me sufficient positive feedback about by work	1	2	3	4	5
31.	My supervisor asks me for input into decisions or to solve problems	1	2	3	4	5
32.	I get enough recognition from senior management for work well done	1	2	3	4	5
33.	When I first started this job, I received the orientation I needed	1	2	3	4	5
34.	The mandatory workshops at (organization) are necessary	1	2	3	4	5
35.	The training received in the mandatory workshops helps me do my job	1	2	3	4	5
36.	(organization) provides me with sufficient other training and workshops	1	2	3	4	5
37.	I like the work that I do	1	2	3	4	5
38.	I am proud to work for (organization)	1	2	3	4	5
39.	I feel I am valued by (organization)	1	2	3	4	5
40.	Written communication keeps me informed about what's going on	1	2	3	4	5
41.	Written communication happens often enough	1	2	3	4	5
42.	Face to face communication with coordinators happens often enough	1	2	3	4	5

Any comments relating to this page?

		Disagree Strongly				Agree Strongly
43.	I feel I can trust what my supervisor tells me	1	2	3	4	5
44.	I feel I can trust what my coordinator tells me	1	2	3	4	5
45.	Providing high quality service is a top priority at (organization)	1	2	3	4	5
46.	There is a spirit of cooperation at (organization)	1	2	3	4	5
47.	I have sufficient opportunity to participate in making decisions that may impact on me	1	2	3	4	5
48.	I have a sense of belonging to the association as a whole	1	2	3	4	5
49.	I understand the long-term plans of (organization)	1	2	3	4	5
50.	I have sufficient opportunity to participate in the planning processes at (organization)	1	2	3	4	5
51.	I have confidence in the senior management team	1	2	3	4	5
52.	I have confidence in the Board of Directors	1	2	3	4	5
53.	My wage is fair for my responsibilities	1	2	3	4	5
54.	I am happy with the benefits I receive	1	2	3	4	5

Any comments relating to this page?

		Disagree Strongly			Agree Strongly	
55.	I am satisfied with the amount of vacation time I receive	1	2	3	4	5
56.	I am satisfied with the amount of Heath Care paid by (organization)	1	2	3	4	5
57.	I am satisfied with the amount of sick leave I receive	1	2	3	4	5
58.	I would like to participate in a savings plan	1	2	3	4	5
59.	I am satisfied with the life insurance provided	1	2	3	4	5
60.	I am satisfied with the short term disability benefits available	1	2	3	4	5
61.	I am satisfied with the long term disability benefits available	1	2	3	4	5
62.	I am satisfied with the dental plan	1	2	3	4	5
63.	I am satisfied with the accidental death and dismemberment benefits available	1	2	3	4	5
64.	I am satisfied with the extended health benefits (prescription drugs, ambulance, etc.)	1	2	3	4	5
65.	Sharing costs of benefits 50/50 by the employee and (organization) is reasonable	1	2	3	4	5
66.	I feel I understand the benefits I am entitled to	1	2	3	4	5
67.	I feel the current benefits offered me are sufficient for me and my family	1	2	3	4	5

68. Are there any other benefits you would like added?

Any comments relating to this page?

172

		Disagree Strongly			Agree Strongly	
69.	I would like more opportunities to socialize and have fun with my co-workers outside of work (parties, barbecues, etc.)	1	2	3	4	5
70.	I would recommend employment at (organization) to a friend	1	2	3	4	5
71.	Overall I am satisfied with (organization) as an employer	1	2	3	4	5

72. What could be done to increase your satisfaction as a (organization) employee?

73. What part of working for (organization) do you find most satisfying?

74. Any other comments you wish to make?

Thank you for completing the survey. Please mail it in the stamped return envelope *today!* All staff will receive a copy of the summarized results. Deadline for returned surveys is (date).

Appendix 3

Key Factors Influencing Employees' Decisions to Stay
Sample Survey

Instructions

1. Please read each of the 30 items on the list below. <u>Read the entire list now.</u>

2. Now consider which 10 (**and only 10**) items on the list are the <u>most important</u> factors that influence your decision to <u>continue as an employee</u> of (agency).

    Place the numbers 1 through 10 (1 is the most important, 10 is less important) beside the 10 items you chose.   Your responses are confidential and anonymous.

	Fair and reasonable policies and practices
	Support and guidance from my immediate supervisor
	Flexible scheduling of my work hours
	Open communication at all levels
	Wages or salary
	Working hours and/or work days
	Opportunity for promotion
	Benefits (health care, dental, pension, vacation time, family leave, etc.)

	New challenges, opportunities to learn on the job
	Formal training (workshops, courses, etc.)
	Regular feedback about how I am doing
	Support from my coworkers
	Opportunities for input into decisions that affect me
	Trusting senior managers to make good and fair decisions
	A balance of work and home time, or time off
	A sense of community among everyone I work with
	A sense that my work here makes a difference for people or society
	Freedom and trust to decide how I will do my job
	A clear understanding of my duties and role
	Support in resolving problems or conflict
	Being listened to when I have an idea or a problem
	Support and direction when I've made a mistake on the job
	Working as a member of a team
	Organizational values and philosophy that I can believe in (or agree with)
	Support with personal problems from supervisor and/or co-workers
	Variety in the tasks/activities in my job
	Meeting the needs/challenges of the clients we serve

	Coworkers who care about doing their jobs well
	Having the materials, tools, equipment to do my job well
	Having good friends at work
	Knowing my job is secure

I work

- ❑ less than 35 hrs/week on average
- ❑ 35 or more hrs/week on average

I have worked for this organization for

- ❑ less than 6 months
- ❑ 6 – 12 months
- ❑ 1 – 2 years
- ❑ 2 – 3 years
- ❑ 3 or more years

References

Allen, W.R. & Drevs, R.A. & Ruhe, J.A. (1999). Reasons Why College-Educated Women Change Employment. *Journal of Business and Psychology*, 14(1), 77-93.

Armstrong, M. (1999). *A Handbook of Human Resource Management Practice (7th Edition)*. London, UK: Kogan Page Limited.

Blankertz, L.E., & Robinson, S.E. (1997). Recruitment and Retention of Psychosocial Rehabilitation Workers. *Administration and Policy in Mental Health*, 24(3), 221-234.

Buckingham, M. & Clifton, D.O. (2001). *Now, Discover Your Strengths*. New York, NY: The Free Press.

Buckingham, M. & Coffman, C. (1999). *First, Break all the Rules*. New York, NY: Simon & Schuster.

Cooley, E., & Yovanoff, P. (1996). Supporting Professionals-at-Risk: Evaluating Interventions to Reduce Burnout and Improve Retention of Special Educators. *Exceptional Children*, 62(4), 336-355.

Daniels, A.C. (1999). *Bringing Out the Best in People: How to Apply the Astonishing Power of Positive Reinforcement*. New York, NY: McGraw-Hill.

Dibble, S. (1999). *Keeping Your Valuable Employees: Retention Strategies for Your Organization's Most Important Resource.* New York, NY: John Wiley & Sons, Inc.

Gilley, J.W. & Maycunich, A. (1999). *Beyond the Learning Organization.* Cambridge, MA: Perseus Books.

Glass, J.L. & Riley, L. (1998). *Family Responsive Policies and Employee Retention Following Childbirth.* Social Forces. University of North Carolina Press.

Hartman Ellis, B. & Miller, K.I. (1994). *Supportive Communication Among Nurses: Effects on Commitment, Burnout and Retention.* Health Communication, Arizona State University.

Herman, R.E. (1999). *Keeping Good People: Strategies for Solving the #1 Problem Facing Business Today.* Winchester, VA: Oakhill Press.

Izzo, J.B., & Withers, P. (2000). *Values Shift: The New Work Ethic & What it Means for Business.* Toronto, ON: Prentice Hall Canada.

Kaye, B. & Jordan-Evans, S. (1999). *Love 'em or Lose 'em: Getting Good People to Stay.* San Francisco, CA: Berrett-Koehler Publishers, Inc.

Larson, S.A., & Lakin, K.C., & Bruininks, R.H. (1998*). Staff Recruitment and Retention: Study Results and Intervention Strategies.* American Association on Mental Retardation.

Lauer, S. & Gebhardt, B.J. (1997). *Now Hiring! Finding and Keeping Good Help for Your Entry-Wage Jobs.* New York, NY: AMACOM.

Levesque, J.D. (1996). *Complete Manual for Recruiting, Hiring and Retaining Quality Employees.* Englewood Cliffs, NJ: Prentice Hall.

McDonnell, W.A., & Wilson-Simpson, D. (1994). *Atmosphere Assessment in Residential Treatment.* Haworth Press, Inc.

Outlaw, W. (1998). *Smart Staffing.* Chicago, IL: Upstart Publishing Company.

Poulin, J.E. & Walter, C.A. (1992). Retention Plans and Job Satisfaction of Gerontological Social Workers. *Journal of Gerontological Social Work*, 19(1), 99-114.

Roberts, D.N. & Sarvela, P.D. (1990). Community Care Workers in Rural Southern Illinois: Job Satisfaction and Implications for Employee Retention. *Home Health Care Services Quarterly*, 10(3/4), 93-115.

Sims, R. R., & Veres III, J.G. (ed.). (1999). *Keys to Employee Success in Coming Decades.* Westport, CT: Quorum Books.

Smith, P., & Schiller, M.R., & Grant, H.K. & Sachs, L. (1995).
Recruitment and Retention Strategies Used by
Occupational Therapy Directors in Acute Care,
Rehabilitation, and Long-Term Care Settings.
American Journal of Occupational Therapy, 49(5), 412-
419.

Spector, P. E.(2000). *Industrial and Organizational
Psychology: Research and Practice*, Second Edition.
New York, NY: John Wiley & Sons, Inc.

Taunton, R.L. & Boyle, D.K. & Woods, C.Q. & Hansen, H.E. &
Bott, M.J. (1997). Manager Leadership and Retention
of Hospital Staff Nurses. *Western Journal of Nursing
Research,* 19(2), 205-225.

Vocational and Rehabilitation Research Institute (2000),
Staff Turnover in Services to Persons with
Developmental Disabilities in Alberta – Survey
Findings. Calgary, AB.

Book Order Form

Name _____ Tel (___) _____

Organization _____ Fax (___) _____

E-mail _____

Address _____

City/Town _____ Prov ____ PC _____

PLEASE SEND:

_____ Great Boards – Plain and Simple @ $24.95   = $_____
_____ Great Boards – The Workbook @ $9.95   = $_____
_____ Supervisors Big Book of Answers @ $19.95   = $_____
_____ Taming Turnover @ $19.95   = $_____

Sub-total (A)	$ _____
Shipping & Handling (see chart)	$ _____
Sub-total	$ _____
Minus Volume Discount (see chart)	-(_____)
Sub-total	$ _____
Plus 7 % GST	$ _____
Total Order Amount	$ _____

METHOD OF PAYMENT:

❑ Visa _____
    Name on Card _____ exp ____ / ____
❑ Purchase Order # _____
❑ Cheque enclosed

THREE CONVENIENT WAYS TO ORDER:

By Phone/Fax:	780 423 3032 (Visa or P.O # Required)
Secure Online Ordering:	www.mmcs.ca (Visa Required)
By Mail:	MMCS/Silver Creek Press
	9741 101A St
	Edmonton, Alberta
	T5K 2R5

> **Orders normally shipped in 24 hours!**

SHIPPING AND HANDLING:

Sub-Total (A)	Add
Up to $20	$4.00
$21 - $40	$7.00
$41 – $60	$8.00
$61 - $80	$9.00
$81 - $120	$10.00
$121 & over	FREE

PUBLISHER DIRECT DISCOUNTS

Order	Subtract
10 – 20 books	5%
21 – 30 books	10%
31 – 40 books	15%
40 – 49 books	20%
50+ books	30%

Any combinations of titles

Book Order Form

Name _____ Tel (　　) _____

Organization _____ Fax (　　) _____

E-mail _____

Address _____

City/Town _____ Prov ____ PC _____

PLEASE SEND:

____Great Boards – Plain and Simple @ $24.95　　= $_____

____Great Boards – The Workbook @ $9.95　　　　= $_____

____Supervisors Big Book of Answers @ $19.95　= $_____

____Taming Turnover @ $19.95　　　　　　　　　= $_____

Sub-total (A)	$ _____
Shipping & Handling (see chart)	$ _____
Sub-total	$ _____
Minus Volume Discount (see chart)	-(_____)
Sub-total	$ _____
Plus 7 % GST	$ _____
Total Order Amount	$_____

METHOD OF PAYMENT:

❑　Visa _____

　　Name on Card _____ exp ____ / ____

❑　Purchase Order # _____

❑　Cheque enclosed

THREE CONVENIENT WAYS TO ORDER:

By Phone/Fax:	780 423 3032 (Visa or P.O # Required)
Secure Online Ordering:	www.mmcs.ca (Visa Required)
By Mail:	MMCS/Silver Creek Press
	9741 101A St
	Edmonton, Alberta
	T5K 2R5

> ## Orders normally shipped in 24 hours!

SHIPPING AND HANDLING:

Sub-Total (A)	Add
Up to $20	$4.00
$21 - $40	$7.00
$41 – $60	$8.00
$61 - $80	$9.00
$81 - $120	$10.00
$121 & over	FREE

PUBLISHER DIRECT DISCOUNTS

Order	Subtract
10 – 20 books	5%
21 – 30 books	10%
31 – 40 books	15%
40 – 49 books	20%
50+ books	30%

Any combinations of titles